8 to 80

The Next 1,000% Stocks and Trends Everyone Can Ride

Howard Lindzon and Ivaylo Ivanov

Charles Street Publishing
819 N. Charles Street
Baltimore, MD 21201
Phone: 1-800-583-0428
www.laughtradeprofit.com

ISBN: 978-0-692-91136-5

Printed in the United States of America

To my wife Ellen and my kids Rachel and Max, thanks for making my job easy. To all the people who encourage me to share ideas, this book is for you. To all the people that have trusted me with their investing capital, thanks for the support and the opportunity to do something I love. And to anyone new to investing…just get started!

— Howard Lindzon

To all eight-year-olds who will probably get to live to 160 in the next century. To all 80-year-olds who still have an eight-year-old's excitement for life. Also, to my family, girlfriend, and friends who might read this book. Investing is a language that can be learned and a skill that can provide life-long benefits and joy.

— Ivaylo Ivanov

CONTENTS

PREFACE

By Joshua M. Brown

What do you do when you constantly find yourself in the presence of brilliant people?

You're certainly not going to out-brilliant them. In the world that Howard Lindzon inhabits, this is an ongoing issue. He knows all of the best and brightest entrepreneurs and executives, from Silicon Valley to Wall Street, and he frequently finds himself in the company of genius.

Howard's solution to this conundrum is what this book is about. Rather than trying to be the smartest person in the room, he has succeeded in becoming the most clever. And cleverness, it should be noted, is oftentimes better than being smart. After all, isn't it true that it takes a clever person to notice that moment when all of the smart people are either onto something big or getting things very, very wrong?

Howard's cleverness in the presence of all his brilliant friends and contacts is a sort of genius unto itself. Since the 1990s he's been at the forefront of picking up on major trends and being early to some of the biggest changes in markets and financial technology. He has consistently kept up to speed with where things were headed. By being open-minded and extraordinarily well connected, he hasn't missed a trick.

More importantly, Howard has never hesitated to share the valuable insights that his travels and conversations have yielded. His followers, business partners, and acquaintances love this generosity, and they have reciprocated tenfold over the years.

I first met Howard in 2009 after the attention my new blog was getting had popped up on his radar screen. I was invited to an early StockTwits get-together in lower Manhattan and persuaded a couple of friends to come along with me.

I knew no one in the FinTech world and financial social media was in its infancy. Virtually no one was using social media to discuss finance and investing at the time. We were in the depths of the Great Financial Crisis and this universe of early adopters was tiny. The cognoscenti was comprised of some day-traders, several venture capitalists, a handful of market reporters and a few tech weirdos.

Howard and I only spoke for a few moments, but as I watched the scene unfold around me, I knew that this was my chance to take whatever talent I may have possessed and see if there might be a business opportunity.

Within a few months, Howard and the StockTwits community were promoting and supporting my writing and social sharing in a way that no one had ever had in my whole life. They asked nothing in return other than for me to be myself and to "be awesome." I had never experienced anything like it, and I immediately became an apostle for the Lindzon ethos.

This idea that smart people from different disciplines could band together, support each other's' efforts, become friends and ride mega-trends together in the investment markets and in life — it was intoxicating.

Soon after our initial conversation, Howard invited me to his Lindzonpalooza event on Coronado Island in San Diego. I was in a bad place financially and career-wise — so much so that I almost had to borrow the money to pay for the flights and a room at the Hotel del Coronado. Howard insisted I come out and network. It was there that I met one of my heroes (and current business partner), Barry Ritholtz, and my entire life changed. I'm not the only person in Howard's orbit that has a story about some career- or life-altering connection being made because of him.

Readers of this book are in for a treat. It's the rare person who can speak knowledgeably and from experience about building companies, investing for profit and joy, spotting trends early and navigating the markets, both public and private. My friend Howard Lindzon has been doing all of these things for decades.

More than this, he has done so in a more entertaining way than anyone else I can think of. His ability to make investing and entrepreneurship fun has garnered him thousands of friends, followers and well-wishers from coast to coast. I'm proud to call myself one of them.

I hope you enjoy this clever little book, from one of the most clever people in the game.

Joshua M. Brown
Merrick, New York
"Downtown" Josh Brown of *The Reformed Broker*
(www.thereformedbroker.com)

INTRODUCTION

No One Is Too Small to Succeed or Too Big to Fail

The quality of our lives depends on the decisions we make every day.

The best return you'll ever get is from investing in yourself. But not everyone has a brilliant idea and, more importantly, the means, the skills, and the desire to build a great business.

Let's be real: How many of us could actually create the next Facebook, Apple, Nike, or Tesla?

Warren Buffett says that he'd rather own a small part of a wonderful company than 100% of a so-so business.

There's nothing sweeter than making your money work for you.

Everyone could invest in companies with great potential and participate in their growth. The stock market gives you that opportunity.

But you have to know how to play the game. And that starts with learning how to speak its language.

If your goal is to achieve average market returns, just consistently put money into low-cost index funds and be done with it. That's a passive strategy, one that more and more investors are adopting.

There is another way to go about it — an active strategy. It requires a much greater commitment. And if you're going to spend time, effort, and money learning how to invest, you want to be sure it's worth it.

3

Indeed, the only reason to actively pick stocks is to achieve returns that will make a real, positive impact on your life and the life of your family.

We do it for profit, and we do it for joy.

There are no sure things in the stock market. Nothing is promised or guaranteed, to anyone. Yet every decade, like clockwork, the market delivers thousands of incredible opportunities for fantastic returns.

We like to invest in growth stocks. Growth is good, but it can also be scary. It comes in various forms.

We love finding underfollowed gems with huge potential. There's nothing better than jumping on a stock at $10 when no one is paying attention and selling near $100 when it's making front-page headlines.

But we also appreciate established companies with huge moats. We call them "8 to 80" brands because their products and services are often used by several generations.

When the market is in "turmoil" we like to go shopping for these types of stocks.

Sometimes Apple is the next Apple, and a well-known company can reward its investors for decades.

This is not a book dedicated to a single company or a particular stock.

In its original form we called it *The Next Apple*. But it could just as easily and accurately have been titled *The Next Amazon*, *The Next Google*, or *The Next Facebook*.

What we do is explain the common characteristics of the best-performing stocks of all time. And we show you how to profit from that knowledge.

The next Apple — or the next Amazon or the next Google or the next Facebook — could and should change your life.

The good news is that over the next 10 years — during any 10-year period, in fact — hundreds of stocks will generate returns of 1,000% or more.

The principles we describe will improve your odds of finding these stocks and riding them until it makes a substantial difference in your life.

When you're done reading this book, you'll be a smarter, more focused investor.

Here's a brief overview of the questions we answer.

- How can we find the next big stock market winners and ride them for a 1,000% percent returns? It's not easy, and it might be psychologically impossible for many of us. But there is a proven way to do it.

- "Follow your passion" is frequently given advice. Is "invest in what you love and use every day" an equally bright idea?

- How do we invest in recent IPOs for 100% gains?

- Does past performance impact future returns? The answer might surprise you, and it might also change the way you invest.

- How do we find the best-performing stocks in any given year? Hard as it may be, we can't expect to achieve superior results if we do what everyone else does.

- Timing is everything. When is the absolute best time to buy, and which stocks should we buy?

- The market is an opportunity machine. Some trends last only several quarters before they fade, while others continue for years and deliver fantastic returns. How can we hold our winning stocks long enough to make a difference?

- Sooner or later, every trend ends. This is not an opinion. It is a fact. When is the right time to sell a stock?

The only question that will remain is whether you'll use the knowledge from this book to create a better life for you and your family.

Please join us at www.laughtradeprofit.com, where we hope you'll invest along with Peloton, our investment advisory service focused on helping people like you find profit and joy.

Howard Lindzon
Ivaylo Ivanov

ONE

Could Apple Be the Next Apple?

*"It is the anticipation of future earnings that
excites people, not the reality."*

— Nicolas Darvas

Apple's Unique Growth Path

In 2003, Apple was a $10 billion company. As of March 2017, Apple is a $755 billion corporation. That's a 75-fold difference.

It's difficult to remember how far Apple had fallen prior to Steve Jobs' return. In the roaring '90s, when technology stocks were all the rage and just the extension ".com" guaranteed at least a billion-dollar valuation, Apple — the company that pioneered the personal computer — was a $3 billion dollar entity on the brink of bankruptcy.

Its annual losses exceeded $1 billion, and its share of the PC market had shrunk to 4%. After rotating three CEOs, the board members tried to sell the company but found no buyers.

In 1997 Microsoft came to the rescue and invested $150 million in Apple. Two months after Apple's deal with Microsoft, Michael Dell told a tech industry conference that if he ran Apple, he'd "shut it down and give the money back to shareholders."

Steve Jobs returned as interim CEO of Apple in September 1997. On a split-adjusted basis, Apple was trading at 80 cents per share at the time. It took Jobs and his team four years to release the first iPod. On the day of iPod's announcement, Apple was trading at $1.30 (adjusted for a 7-for-1 split).

By 2004, many vocal skeptics and disbelievers still doubted Apple's comeback.

Money magazine ran a story headlined "Why iPod Can't Save Apple."

Apple hit a new three-year high at $2 (on a split-adjusted basis), and it never looked back. By the end of 2005, it was trading above $10.

And now it's the most valuable company in the world.

The Next Apple?

There are two major ways a stock could appreciate from a long-term perspective.

One is for the underlying company to grow earnings. The other is to expand its price-to-earnings multiple, which is the price people are willing to pay for a company's earnings.

The first depends primarily on a company's ability to execute, along with external factors such as competition and regulation. The second is almost entirely influenced by market sentiment.

Could Apple — the stock — become the next Apple? Could one of the best-performing stocks of the past 15 years become one of the best-performing stocks of the next decade? If history is a good guide, it's very unlikely.

The biggest stock market winners from decade to decade are very different because of three main factors:

- The Law of Big Numbers
- The Law of High Expectations
- The Law of Innovation

The Law of Big Numbers

Companies are worth a multiple of their earnings, and that multiple is often directly related to earnings growth rates. When you're growing rapidly, you're worth more. When people expect you to grow faster in the future, you're worth more to them today.

Growing earnings and growing expectations at a high pace forever have one thing in common: You can't do it.

Sooner or later, a fast-growing company becomes a slow-growing company. The market often anticipates that and starts to pay lower and lower multiples before there's evidence of actual slowdown. When this happens, the company's stock price begins to decline.

Growing at 100% when your sales are $10 billion is a lot harder than growing at 100% when your top line is $20 million.

It's simply impossible to compound at such a rate for more than several years unless you start from a very low base and you have serious protection against competition. Very few companies are able to achieve that. This is why most upside trends last only a few quarters.

It takes two to three years for a product to transform from an early adopter's toy to being massively popular. Every product has its natural life cycle. The trick to sustain growth is to reinvest profits in order to find the next great product or to acquire it.

Apple managed to sustain its trend for so long because it was able to come up with a new catalyst every two to three years and to basically create new product categories. It redefined retail, music, computing, communication, entertainment, etc.

Apple's catalysts in the 21st century so far include the following:

- iTunes
- Retail Stores
- The iPod
- The iMac
- The iPhone
- The iPad
- iPay
- The iWatch

The Law of High Expectations

Why is it that the very same company sometimes gets valued at 25 times earnings and sometimes it gets valued at 100 times earnings? It all depends on people's expectations. Not so much expectations about earnings growth, but expectations about making money in that stock.

When a stock has been a really great performer for the past few years, it becomes a household name. It has extreme coverage from the press, social media, and financial analysts. It's a lot more predictable, and it's much more difficult to surprise the market.

When expectations are high and a company can't keep surprising the market, there's very high probability of disappointing. It's a matter of "if," not "when," this happens. And when it does happen, look out.

The market could be generous and occasionally give the benefit of the doubt to companies with great growth potential, but it's not all-forgiving.

If those companies don't start to meet the market's expectations in terms of earnings and sales growth, their stocks are likely to decline substantially. High expectations are even more difficult to sustain than high earnings growth.

There are very few sure things in life. Customer loyalty fades. Competitive advantages disappear. Pricing power goes away. Mind share dissipates. Earnings and sales growth slow down.

In other words, circumstances change. But what we can always count on is that high expectations will eventually mean-revert. Most companies can't accelerate their earnings growth fast enough to counter the decline in the market's expectations.

The Law of Innovation

Chris Dixon, a general partner at the venture capital firm Andreessen Horowitz (also known as a16z), says that large, established companies typically go after good ideas that seem like good ideas to everyone else. Startups and younger, smaller companies go after good ideas that seem like bad ideas to almost everyone else.

Younger, smaller companies are hungrier for success. They have to go after crazy ideas that the big guys aren't going to touch; therefore, they have a greater chance of creating something completely new that's going to disrupt the status quo.

Once they get some traction, they have a couple options:

- Sell to larger companies.

- Go all the way, become the next big thing, and, in the process, create great wealth for their shareholders.

When Google launched in 1998, it was very late to the search engine industry. At the time, search was dominated by large portals like Yahoo and AOL, which thought of search as a loss-leader. Stickiness, or the ability to make people spend more time on your site, was considered the key to business success. Google had the opposite strategy — it was so incredibly good at showing search results that people would immediately leave the website.

Google tried to sell its technology for $1 million to one of the big portals. The CEO of the large portal tried it and said that Google's search engine worked too well and would make people leave its site too quickly.

Google had amazing technology, which was considered a very contrarian business idea that none of the established leaders at the time wanted to try.

Google had no clue how it would make money at the time, but it clearly figured it out.

The takeaway here is that big companies are working hard on good ideas that look like good ideas. They want to bet on a sure thing. When you're so big and have something to lose, you give priority to safety. You only need to get rich once, says Warren Buffett.

If you realize this, you're going to do things very differently. You won't take on big risks. You won't risk something that's important to you for something that's not that essential. This is exactly how most big companies think.

A company that's already been successful for quite some time and has grown into a giant isn't likely to develop the next big revolutionary technology. Large corporations are interested in keeping the status quo and continuing to enjoy their market-leader status. They often innovate through acquisitions, but those acquisitions rarely have big impacts on market leaders' top and bottom lines.

For example, when Google acquired YouTube for $1.6 billion in late 2006, it had already gone up 500% since its first trading day as a public company. By all measures, YouTube has been an amazing purchase, but since its acquisition, Google stock has gone up only 180% in the 10 years since. Most of its gain came after 2013.

Even if a big company is proactive and innovative, the resulting new products or services are rarely game-changers for its earnings and sales growth. Apple did it with the iPhone, but Apple is an exception that was run by a visionary genius who wasn't afraid to make bold moves.

Coke and Pepsi didn't initially go after the energy drink market. Red Bull and Monster Beverage did, and they delivered incredible returns for their investors.

The Walkman had huge success, but its impact on Sony's bottom line was minimal. The iPod had huge impact for Apple when it was a small company trying to redefine the way we consume music.

The iWatch came out at a time when Apple was already the biggest company in the world. The iWatch has made Apple several billion dollars since its release in 2015. Several billion dollars is a lot of money, but it is almost irrelevant for Apple's current revenue size.

Its overall impact has been too small to move the needle and accelerate Apple's growth.

The First Trillion-Dollar Company

Apple is likely to be the first company to ever reach a market cap of $1 trillion. In early 2017, it's almost there.

Our goal as investors should not be to find a stock that will go from $750 billion to $1 trillion, but to own the next stocks that will go from $1 billion to $50 billion, from $200 million to $20 billion or from $5 billion to $100 billion in market cap.

Apple, Google, Amazon, and Baidu are well-known and established companies in 2017. But 15 to 20 years ago, they were either still private companies or fast-growing risky bets that not many were willing to take. The market didn't know how to properly price them. They had many skeptics and doubters.

No one had any idea that they would reward their early shareholders so generously.

The next Apple and the next Google are not likely to be the current Apple and the current Google. Ten years from now both companies will still have an enormous impact on many people's everyday lives. They'll probably still be extremely profitable companies, but they won't go up 100 times, or even 10 times, from their current levels.

The market is always the same because the market is always different. The names of the big winners change every three to five years — sometimes even more often — but they all go through similar paths. Studying their identical patterns could help us immensely in finding the next stocks that are likely to go up 200% in a year or 1,000% in five years.

The vast majority of big, long-term trends start with a breakout to new 52-week highs from a proper base. The underlying reasons behind this breakout could be very different.

Big trends start in two main ways.

In the first case, price momentum leads and earnings are expected to catch up later. Here the market is forward-looking. Stocks could break out to new 52-week highs when earnings are either not existent yet or very low and the market is willing to pay crazy high price-to-earnings multiple for them.

This is the story of the vast majority of momentum stocks.

Apple, Google, Amazon, Baidu, and hundreds of others have traveled the same path. The market gave them very generous premiums at the beginning of their price cycles, but those companies were able to meet and even exceed expectations later by delivering solid earnings growth for prolonged periods.

Thus, it's the anticipation of future earnings — not the reality — that often drives investing in growth stocks.

In the second case, earnings growth leads, price momentum follows. Sometimes the stock market is slow to react to a big change in earnings, especially when it doesn't involve a popular name in a sexy industry. Prices change when expectations change.

Big, long-term trends often start with a sudden explosion in earnings that alters the market's expectations.

Many of the best long-term market performers belong to this group — including Monster Beverage, The Middleby Corporation, Keurig Mountain Coffee, and Home Depot.

Great Growth Stories Are Never Cheap

Fast-growing companies are rare, and they always trade at premium valuations. Very few exciting growth stories emerge every year compared to the thousands of institutions that want to own them.

A lot of money is chasing a small number of great stocks. Of course, the market will sometimes overreact and push prices to levels that seem unjustified at the time. No one wants to miss the next Tesla, Google, Apple, or Chipotle Mexican Grill.

Investors with a bias against stocks with high price-to-earnings ratios (or P/E ratio) miss some of the greatest stock market winners of all time.

The P/E ratio line of many long-term market winners ends up being downward slopping. The relationship of price to earnings reflects the market's expectations for near-term growth. It's normal for a stock that grows earnings at 100% to trade at more than 100 times its earnings per share. It's also normal for market expectations to decline over time and, therefore, a P/E ratio to become a double-digit figure.

If a company manages to grow its earnings faster than market expectations decline, it will see its stock appreciate over time. The truth, however, is that very few companies are able to achieve high earnings growth for more than a few quarters. This is why most trends last only a few quarters. You could still make a lot of money riding those trends, but a real long-term stock winner is made by its earnings.

Consider the following growth stories.

Apple

A long-term trend inevitably climbs a wall of worry. Every trend benefits from a healthy portion of skeptics and disbelievers, as they are signs there's someone left to buy.

The story of Apple the company has remained the same for the past 15 years: It makes great products that people love and desire to have.

The story of Apple the stock, meanwhile, has changed dramatically.

Figure 1-1

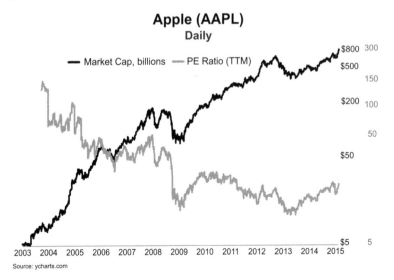

Apple (AAPL)
Daily

Source: ycharts.com

Apple grew its earnings at a 200% rate as recently as 2004, and the market was glad to pay 100 times earnings for its stock. As Apple grew bigger and bigger, investors grew more and more skeptical about the company's ability to sustain its growth rate.

Apple managed to outgrow people's skepticism by sustaining impressive growth numbers for a long period of time.

Between the end of 2004 and 2014, Apple's market cap increased 31 times. Its earnings growth was even more impressive — 126 times. Earnings growth was offset by an 80% decline in the price-to-earnings multiple that the market was willing to pay.

Figure 1-2

Apple, Inc.	2014	2004	Difference
EPS	$6.45	$0.05	126.5X
Revenue	$183 B	$8.3 B	22X
Market Cap	$700 B	$22.5 B	31X

Blackberry

When it comes to smart phones today, most people think of Apple, Google, Samsung, and maybe China-based Xiaomi. Fifteen years ago, the kings of mobile were Nokia and Research in Motion, better known by what it called its devices, BlackBerry.

In 2003, BlackBerries were ubiquitous in Corporate America, and they were just starting to appeal to Main Street. Research in Motion was still an undiscovered $1 billion company that was losing money despite generating $300 million in annual sales.

Figure 1-3

Blackberry (BBRY)
Daily

— Market Cap, billions — PE Ratio (TTM)

Source: ycharts.com

Its stock cleared new 52-week highs and went from $5 to $150 in five years. Then, in the following four years, it declined 95%. It looked expensive all the way up, and it looked cheap for a good portion of its downward move. BlackBerry started as a very expensive stock, but it managed to justify the market's high expectations.

Google

When it completed its initial public offering in 2004, Google was a $40 billion dollar company with a P/E ratio of 130 on earnings per share of $2. By 2015 Google had become a $390 billion dollar company on annual earnings of $20 per share with a P/E ratio of 28.

Its earnings went up about 10 times. Its stock is also up about 10 times for the same period. The difference is in the P/E ratio, which basically measures the market's expectations.

Figure 1-4

Google (GOOGL)
Daily

— Market Cap, billions   — PE Ratio (TTM)

Source: ycharts.com

In 2004, Google was a young company that was consistently posting over 100% quarterly earnings growth. It was absolutely justified
to trade at a high P/E multiple. High growth is rare, and financial
markets reward it generously.

As Google became a giant and its growth slowed down, though,
the market's expectations declined correspondingly. Analysts expect
Google earnings to grow 18% in 2017.

Baidu

Speaking of search engines, the biggest one in China has returned
its investors even more money than Google.

Baidu went public in 2005 at $27 per share, which is $2.70 on a
split-adjusted basis. (The stock split 10-for-1 in 2010.) It was considered the hottest IPO of the year. Baidu gained 350% on its first trading
day, finishing at $112.5 (that's $12.25 split-adjusted).

Baidu has never looked cheap over the past decade. It traded at
high P/E multiples all the way from a split-adjusted $2.70 to $220.

There's an important lesson here: Don't be afraid to pay up for high-growth stocks with great potential.

Figure 1-5

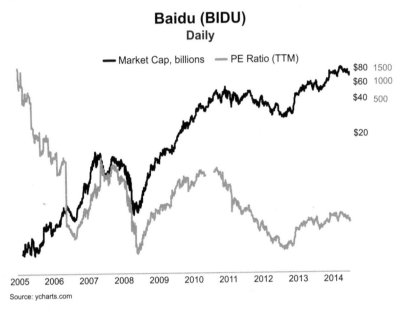

Baidu (BIDU)
Daily

In many cases they're expensive for a reason. Over time, earnings could more than catch up with people's expectations and justify high valuations.

This is exactly what happened with Baidu. In the quarter before its IPO it earned $8 million. In its last quarter for 2014 Baidu earned $565 million.

To paraphrase Benjamin Graham, over the short term the market is a voting machine, and over the long term it's a weighing machine.

At some point, valuation matters — but only if earnings don't catch up, you plan to hold forever, and you don't have an exit strategy. If price gets you in a trade or investment, price should take you out. If you don't know why you bought, you won't know when to sell.

Big Earnings Explosions Create Big Trends

Financial markets strive to be forward-looking, but that's not the case when it comes to underfollowed small-cap stocks in obscure industries.

Such stocks remain under the radar of most investors until they report huge acceleration in earnings growth. When a company that used to grow at 5% to 10% suddenly reports a 300% increase in earnings and a 100% increase in sales, it will grab the attention of many investors. It also will likely gap 10 to 50% to new multi-year highs.

The good news is that this is often the beginning of a new powerful trend, not the end. Monster Beverage is a good representative of this category.

Figure 1-6

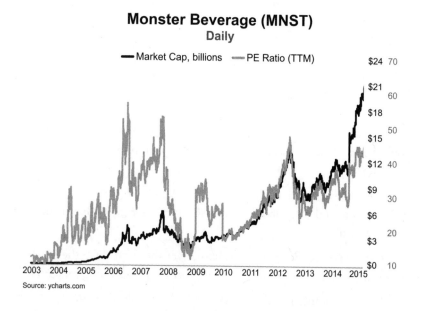

Monster Beverage (MNST)
Daily

Source: ycharts.com

A high-growth, underfollowed stock like Monster is likely to go through three main stages:

- Earnings growth leads price growth. There is a sudden, major acceleration in earnings growth that starts a process of re-pricing. Since the stock in question is still underfollowed, the market is likely to react slowly and under-discount this new, potentially disruptive trend. Most investors are still cautious with the new name. Either they don't trust the sustainability of the story yet or they haven't heard about it. A single quarter with big expansion in earnings is like a cockroach: There is never only one.

- After a few much-better-than-expected quarters and major price appreciation, it becomes a momentum stock. Price starts to appreciate faster than earnings grow — the P/E multiple of the stock expands. At this stage, the stock and its story are widely known and understood. The market projects current levels of growth into infinity, and it proactively discounts the best-case scenario.

- There are two scenarios in stage three:

  o P/E multiple drops: Price growth decelerates to the level of earnings growth, and both start to go hand and hand.

  o P/E multiple crashes: Price growth drops below the level of earnings growth, which indicates a major correction — this is typical for most momentum stocks.

Growing Under the Radar

Some of the best long-term performers in the market are boring, under-the-radar businesses that grow 10% to 20% a year, pay regular dividends, and have the power to easily pass rising costs to customers.

The stocks of such companies rarely trade too cheaply to attract the attention of value investors. And because they belong to a boring industry that can't grab the attention of the media and fascinate investors about their potential future, they rarely become momentum stocks.

They aren't going to follow the typical pattern of a hot momentum name — go up 200% to 800% in a couple years only to quickly give back 50% to 90% of it. Their stocks are likely to rise much more gradually but also much more consistently. Their price appreciation will track their earnings growth, and sentiment will have much smaller impact.

Earnings growth comes from two major sources:

- attracting more customers to spend more money; and

- pricing power — the ability to raise prices faster than the increase in your costs. As Warren Buffett says, "If you have to light candles every time you raise prices by 10%, you are in the wrong business."

Costco Wholesale, Middleby Corporation, and O'Reilly Automotive are good examples that have fit this description.

Costco has managed to grow its annual earnings by 10% to 20% for most of the period from 1995 to 2015. Its stock went up 2000% in a 20-year period. Further, $1,000 invested in the 1982 Costco IPO is worth about $170,000 in 2017. Not too bad for a boring retailer.

Figure 1-7

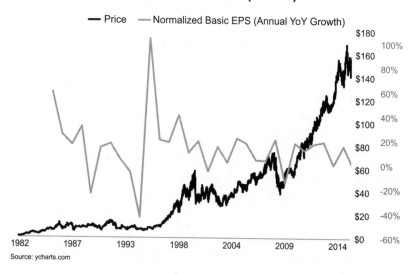

Costco Wholesale (COST)

Source: ycharts.com

Middleby has a similar story — but with a twist. During the Gold Rush, most gold-seekers didn't make much money. Whatever they made, they spent.

The great wealth was created by those who supplied the miners with food, clothes, tools, and entertainment. The same business model continues to work flawlessly, to this very day.

Figure 1-8

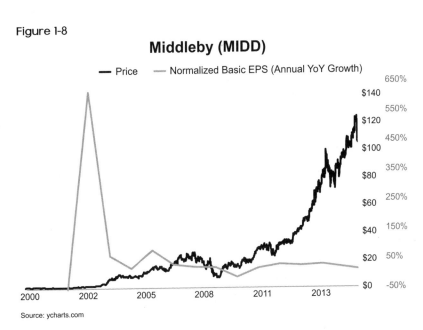

Source: ycharts.com

Middleby sells restaurant equipment. Most restaurants could only dream of Middleby's returns.

From 1993 to 2015, Middleby stock went from a split-adjusted 50 cents per share to $107, a 214-fold increase. Restaurants as a group haven't been a bad long-term investment, either.

According to Worden, the group is up 1,800% since 1989, which is three times the S&P 500's performance.

And then there's O'Reilly Automotive. Could there be anything more trivial than selling auto parts? It's a boring but very lucrative business.

Figure 1-9

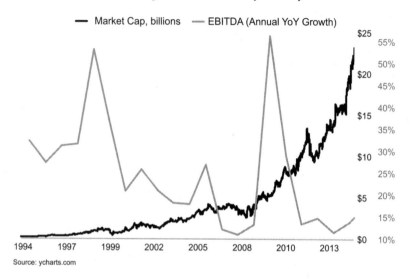

O'Reilly Automotive (ORLY)

— Market Cap, billions   — EBITDA (Annual YoY Growth)

Source: ycharts.com

O'Reilly Automotive has grown its earnings by 20% annually for most of the past 22 years (1992 through 2015). The result? An 8,600% return for its investors.

A Word to the Wise

Every study of past winners should be taken with a grain of salt because it has the inevitable element of survivorship bias.

For each Amazon, Apple, and Google, there are 50 others that didn't make it. Unfortunately, we can't study the future. Past data is all we have.

Having a clue about the major traits that stocks should possess in order to have a chance to become big future winners is necessary but insufficient.

Comprehending risk management is just as important, and we cover it in later chapters.

TWO

Perception Is Reality

*"The market is better at predicting the news
than the news is at predicting the market."*

— Gerald Loeb

The Stock Market Is Forward-Looking,
Most of the Time

The stock market has its own rules — rules that might seem counterintuitive to many. Stocks with incredible fundamentals could go down 50% or more during market corrections. Stocks without any earnings can go up 500% in a bull market.

The allure of future earnings — not the reality — is what often drives investors' decision-making.

Some trends are based on solid fundamentals. Others are based on wishful thinking. A good story about a tremendous future could substantially push up a stock price very quickly. It's not too unusual to see several-hundred-percent moves in a few quarters. The anticipation of growth rather than the growth itself could lead to great profits in growth stocks.

In 2012-13, Yelp was perceived to be at the perfect crossroads of three of the hottest trends at the time: mobile, social, and local. Its shares tripled before it reported its first profitable quarter.

Figure 2-1

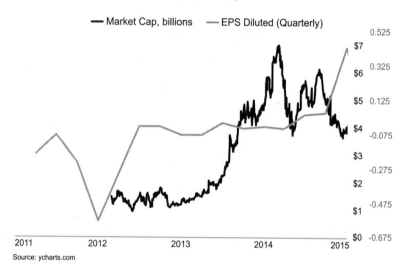

Yelp (YELP)

— Market Cap, billions   — EPS Diluted (Quarterly)

Source: ycharts.com

Tesla went from $30 to $300 in 2013-14 without a single profitable quarter. In fact, its founder and CEO, Elon Musk, warned the market that Tesla will reinvest its operating earnings and that it probably won't report any earnings based on Generally Accepted Accounting Principles (GAAP) before 2020.

Early adopters loved its new car. In many people's eyes, Tesla was doing for the car industry what Apple had done for the computer and smartphone industries. The market gave Tesla the benefit of the doubt. It discounted a bright future.

Of course, there's always a chance that its stock might turn out to be a flop, but that doesn't mean that you will have to give back most of your profits.

Figure 2-2

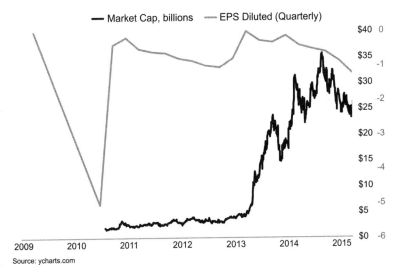

Tesla (TSLA)

— Market Cap, billions   — EPS Diluted (Quarterly)

Source: ycharts.com

BlackBerry quadrupled before reporting its first profitable quarter in 2003. At the time, its revolutionary products were taking over Corporate America, and it was only a matter of time before households jumped on the train, too.

Anyone who waited for those companies to report their first profitable quarter before buying missed out on substantial gains. Anyone who waited for those stocks to become reasonably valued before buying missed out on their entire moves.

Those three stocks — Yelp, Tesla, and BlackBerry — are not exceptions. They represent the typical story of many momentum stocks.

Just because a company isn't making money today, it doesn't mean it won't start making money tomorrow. You should always ask yourself what the reason is behind the lack of current profits.

Is it a flawed business model that is not likely to be fixed? Or is it because the company is heavily investing today to make a lot more money tomorrow?

Financial markets live in the future. They constantly strive to price events that haven't happened yet. Sometimes, they're spot on and discount what will actually happen ahead of time.

For example, housing and home improvement stocks started to break out to 52-week highs in late 2012 — long before economic data confirmed a housing recovery in the U.S. The market correctly predicted what was going to happen. By the time it was clear that the market had been right all along, most of the upside move in homebuilders was over.

By pricing events that haven't happened yet, financial markets will occasionally discount events that will never happen. Markets aren't always right. A stock could quintuple based solely on investors' speculations and expectations for future profits.

For example, additive manufacturing stock 3D Systems went from $10 to $100 between 2012 and 2013. At the time, the whole world was excited about the possibilities that 3D printing could bring to manufacturing.

Figure 2-3

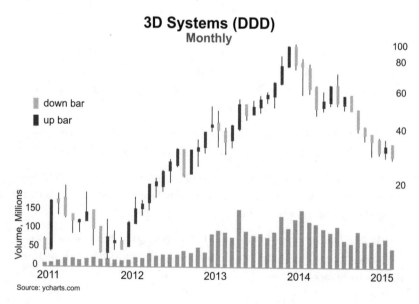

Source: ycharts.com

3D Systems failed to live up to expectations. The market became tired of waiting for the company to start making real money, and it sold the stock off in 2014.

Short-term price moves are based on sentiment. Long-term moves are based on earning power. The story, or, more precisely, the expectations, about a company have to come true at some point. Otherwise, disillusioned market participants will start to sell.

The market is not always a brilliant, forward-looking mechanism. But it's also neither stupid nor naïve, at least not when given enough time.

From a short-term perspective, it could be all of the above times 10 and create results that are both irrational and unpredictable.

Is the Market Always Right?

That the market is forward-looking doesn't mean it's always right.

George Soros likes to joke that the market has predicted seven of the past two recessions. And he's right. Financial markets will sometimes discount fundamentals that will never become reality.

Prices reflect people's expectations about the future, mostly about the near-term future. To say that the market is always right is to assume that people's expectations about the future always come true. We all know that this is not the case. No one has a crystal ball. People are often wrong.

The market is not always anticipating the future.

There are times when it simply corrects previously incorrect views. The market might be discounting the future, but it's not naïve. It doesn't wait forever. It constantly seeks positive feedback — from a short-term perspective based on price, from a longer-term perspective based on fundamentals.

When expectations are met and exceeded, a trend is likely to continue. If a company doesn't live up to expectations, there is often a swift correction.

Most stocks don't manage to live up to market expectations. This is why market history includes thousands of examples of stocks that run 200% to 300% in a year or two then give back most of it. There are very few stocks that manage to keep up with market expectations in the long run.

The discounting of the future is not a science. Sometimes markets can be very emotional and quite irrational. Markets tend to overreact — to both perceived risks and to perceived opportunities. There are times when the market just goes bonkers and sends prices to levels that can't possibly be justified by any future outcome.

There are times when the fear of missing out trumps the fear of losing. People start to chase, price momentum becomes its own catalyst, and short-sellers are mercilessly squeezed, sending prices higher with unimaginable velocity.

As Paul Tudor Jones likes to say on such occasion, "Fundamentals might be good for the first third or first 50 or 60% of a move, but the last third of a great bull market is typically a blow-off, whereas the mania runs wild and prices go parabolic."

In other words, very few investors are prepared for the last third of a move in a trend, when emotions override all reason.

Why Trends Exist

We know the stock market is often but not always forward-looking. But how does that insight help us as market participants?

Being forward-looking requires the anticipation of future events. Discounting the future is a process, not a short-term event. This makes the existence of trends possible. Trends create opportunities to make a lot while risking very little.

Stocks are just like products. Just like there are different buyers in the different stages of a product cycle, there are different people buying at every stage of a typical growth stock's price cycle. There are innovators, early adopters, early majority, late majority, and laggards.

There are various market participants with different philosophies and reasons to buy.

Some buy early, long before the crowd, because they understand or speculate about the potential impact a company or an industry will have. Some buy when a company is still losing money but has great potential, with a great story behind it.

Some buy when a company breaks out to a new 52-week high from a proper base. This could happen well before a company reports any earnings or an improvement in growth. There are market participants who don't care whether the company is making plush bears or space rockets. As long as its stock price is making new highs, they ride it.

Some buy when there's fear of missing out. Institutions have to put money to work, and they have to choose assets to allocate to. At any given time, there are only a few great growth stories in the market versus thousands of institutions that want to own them. In this case, P/E ratios often don't matter. It's all about catching The Next Big Thing. Trends persist because supply is limited — early buyers aren't eager to sell, and there are plenty of new buyers that would like to participate. There's a scarcity of great growth stories, and Wall Street loves growth.

Some buy when the company reports its first profitable quarter.

Some buy when a company has had several quarters of high growth and has a group of analysts who follow it.

Some buy when a company reaches a certain size.

Some buy because they're forced to cover their early/wrong short position. Every trend needs doubters and skeptics. Otherwise, there wouldn't be anyone left to buy. The existence of substantial short-interest has fueled multiple big trends.

Some buy when a certain market cap is reached. Some large funds can't participate in companies with market caps under $5 billion because they can't accumulate a position big enough to make a difference in their returns. When a company gets from a market cap of $1 billion to $5 billion and continues to deliver solid growth numbers, it will find a whole new set of buyers.

On some occasions, market participants are forced to buy or sell regardless of price, which exaggerates current trends and the impact of newly discovered catalysts.

Take, for example, forced liquidation during market corrections. This occurs when investors sell not necessarily because they want to but because they have to due to margin calls and redemptions from scared clients.

Just like there's "forced selling," there is also forced buying. When speculators bet against a stock and it keeps rising, so-called short-sellers are forced to cover their positions and, in the process, provide the fuel for even higher prices.

Finally, inflows of cash to mutual funds require portfolio managers to buy every month, without regard to price.

How Perceptions Impact Fundamentals

George Soros is known as the "man who broke the Bank of England" in the early 1990s, but his main contribution to the financial world is the theory of reflexivity, which claims the following:

- Prices aren't objective. They're based on people's biased perceptions of the future.
- Biased perceptions define people's buys and sells, so perceptions will influence prices.
- Prices impact perceptions and fundamentals, too.

Soros's reflexivity theory is also a common-sense explanation of why trends exist.

What happens when a stock doubles in a year?

The stock market is considered a feedback mechanism. When prices go up, people assume that their initial investment thesis is right and that their expectations are justified. They buy more and are joined by even more people wanting to participate in the trend. The fear of missing out is ruling the market's behavior.

Higher stock prices mean happy shareholders. Happy shareholders mean a lot of good faith and patience for management. CEOs can make a lot bolder moves, and they are given more time to be right. We've all seen the incredible faith that Amazon's shareholders have in founder and CEO Jeff Bezos.

Eighteen years after its IPO, Amazon still loses money on the occasional quarter because it invests heavily in new projects. Amazon has missed more Wall Street earnings expectations than any other major U.S. corporation, yet its stock keeps showing up on the all-time high list.

Management is an important part of a company's fundamentals. When investors trust and believe management, they're willing to give the underlying company a lot higher P/E multiple.

In other words, investors tend to trust managers who make them money. Earning shareholder trust by delivering them early profits does three key things:

- provides a lot of room for innovation and experimenting;
- helps to manage market expectations; and
- allows focus on long-term goals while the rest of the corporate world is focused on the next quarter's results.

Most companies think about what will change in the next 10 years and try to position their businesses according to their projections and expectations. The truth is that no one knows what the next 10 years will look like and what novelties they're going to bring.

The globe is moving faster than ever. Product cycles are a lot shorter. So is our attention span. Innovation is traveling faster than the speed of sound. We change our minds and preferences very frequently. Billion-dollar companies are made and ruined within the span of a decade. It seems that change is the only constant.

But is it?

Jeff Bezos doesn't think so. He thinks about what will NOT change 10 years from now and builds Amazon's long-term strategy around those constants. Lower prices, great service, faster deliveries, and greater product selection: These are cornerstones that aren't going to change, no matter what. People are not likely to ask to pay more, receive their deliveries slower, have less to choose from, and receive crappy customer service.

This is how you create a sustainable competitive advantage.

A company with highly appreciated stock could use it as a currency to acquire competitors and the best human talent in its respective field, which could make it a lot stronger functionally and operationally.

We see how Google, Facebook, Apple, and Tesla are scooping many of the best engineers in the world. We see how Salesforce.com is incredibly active on the acquisition field.

Better prepared and more motivated people. New and better products. Fewer competitors. These are all factors that actually improve a company's fundamentals, and they all could be derived from higher stock prices. The improved fundamentals attract a completely new set of buyers, which sends prices even higher.

A good story could capture the imagination and change expectations. The dream of future profits — not the reality — is what excites people.

This is how momentum works. But the process doesn't last forever.

People's expectations about the future don't always come true. The market constantly tries to discount events that haven't yet happened. As a result, it will sometimes discount events that will never happen.

The market is forward looking, but, at the same time, it's constantly looking for feedback: from a short-term perspective based on price, from a longer-term perspective based on fundamentals.

Sometimes, expectations turn into a self-fulfilling prophecy and end up impacting fundamentals. More often than not, the discounted future is way too optimistic or way too pessimistic. It's human nature to over-discount identified risks and opportunities.

As a result, most trends last only a few quarters, but knowledgeable investors know how to take advantage of them and protect profits when the inevitable pullbacks come.

THREE

IPOs: Every Finish Line Is the Beginning of a New Race

"The risk comes from not knowing what you are doing."

— Warren Buffett

If You Build It

We don't know if a house is a good long-term investment, but putting money to work in home-improvement stores has been a boon. For example, $5,000 invested in Home Depot on its IPO day in 1981 is worth $30 million in early 2017. How much did your house appreciate over the same period?

The journey of every stock starts with an initial public offering (IPO). IPOs represent the first time private owners sell part of their company to the public, including pension funds, mutual funds, hedge funds, and individual investors. Once a company becomes public, its shares can be traded on secondary stock markets, where everyone can buy and sell them. Familiar names such as Apple, Google, and Tesla are publicly traded companies.

Private companies are owned by their founders, employees, angel investors, and venture capitalists. Just before a company goes public, new shares are issued in the name of the company, which is a separate entity. Those shares are usually sold to the public on the IPO day. Most of the money from the IPO proceeds goes into the company's coffers. Insiders gain a liquid market and the ability to sell after lockup expirations, which typically last from six to 12 months after the IPO.

Why do private companies choose to go public?

- To raise money for expansion, operational costs, and strategic acquisitions. This used to be the main reason to go public. Nowadays, there is plenty of money in private markets for high-growth businesses.

- Proper timing. Companies don't go public when they have to but when they can. When investment bankers are confident in the current ability of the market to absorb supply from an industry, companies use the window to go public at proper valuation.

- To receive a valuation they can't get in private markets. Bull markets can be very generous. The depth of the public markets' liquidity is still unmatched.

- To create a liquid market and an exit opportunity for founders, private investors, and early employees.

Some IPOs provide incredible wealth-building opportunities by letting you participate in the growth of various great businesses.

Let's take a look at the most successful IPOs in the past 30 years. Most of them went up 1,000% within five years of their public debuts.

The Road to a 1,000% Return

The worst thing you can do is to look at Figure 3-1 and assume that buying IPOs is a sure thing. Far from it. Many IPOs turn into disasters for public investors. Don't buy blindly on the IPO day, no matter how much you like the company.

Figure 3-1

Company	Symbol	IPO		Reached 1,000% Return	Valuation	Return Since IPO
		Year	Valuation			
Microsoft	MSFT	1986	$500M	1990	$347B	69,300%
Whole Foods	WFM	1992	$104M	1998	$19.3B	18,400%
Qualcomm	QCOM	1991	$412M	1997	$109B	26,360%
Staples	SPLS	1990	$204M	1995	$107B	52,350%
Express Scripts	EXRX	1992	$92M	1997	$60B	65,100%
IAC Interactive	IACI	1993	$51M	1997	$5B	9,700%
Starbucks	SBUX	1992	$111M	1995	$66.8B	60,000%
Yahoo!	YHOO	1996	$551M	1998	$40.6B	7,270%
Cisco Systems	CSCO	1990	$279M	1992	$139B	50,000%
Amazon	AMZN	1997	$441M	1998	$173B	39,130%
eBay	EBAY	1998	$1.8B	1999	$67.6B	3,660%
Tesla Motors	TSLA	2010	$2.13B	2013	$26B	1,100%
Pacira Pharma	PCRX	2011	$252M	2014	$4.25B	1,600%
SolarCity	SCTY	2012	$768M	2014	$5.13B	560%

When you invest in an IPO, you need to understand your place in the puzzle. There are so many willing suppliers of stocks, including venture capitalists who want to bring back some money after years of waiting, employees who are in a hurry to taste their newly acquired wealth, and investment banks that are looking for a quick flip.

Unless new public companies report much-better-than-expected earnings or have fascinating stories behind them, they often experience deep pullbacks as lockup periods expire.

Investors Have to Adjust Their Expectations for IPOs

A quick walk through recent financial history tells us a lot about the major changes in IPO markets over the past few decades.

In 1980, Nike debuted as a public company by raising $5 million. At that point, Nike was already the biggest athletic shoe company in the U.S., with enviable records of growth and a solid balance sheet.

Today, there are startups without a product or revenue stream that raise more money in private rounds.

Apple's IPO was in December 1980. It sold 4.6 million shares at $22, raising about $100 million. It generated more revenue than any company since Ford's IPO in 1956. It instantly created 300 million-aires. By the end of the day, the stock had increased in value by almost 32% to close at $29, leaving the company with a market capitalization of $1.78 billion.

In 1986 Microsoft raised $63 million by offering 3.1 million shares at $21. It had 24.7 million outstanding shares; its initial market cap was about $500 million. Don't forget that, at the time, Microsoft was already a well-known and extremely profitable company with 11 years of growth behind it.

In the midst of the biggest known bubble in financial history in 1997, Amazon went public at a $440 million valuation.

Do you notice the amounts that those tech giants raised on their IPO days and their initial valuation? They are giants today; they were giants back then — or at least notable leaders in their respective in-dustries.

Today, private companies without any revenues raise more money in private markets.

Nike, Microsoft, Amazon, and similar companies went public relatively early in their growth cycles. As a result, public investors had the opportunity to participate in 95% to 99% of their overall price ap-preciation. Founders, early employees, and venture capitalists took all the risk. Most of the reward was left for grabbing — anyone could've bought those stocks on the secondary markets.

Things have changed in the aftermath of the 2008-09 financial crisis.

The Federal Reserve's accommodative monetary policy and historically low interest rates have combined to push an increasing percentage of capital into risky asset classes like venture capital and "angel investing." This capital has chased up valuations in the pipeline preceding IPOs, making the IPOs feel more like the end of the journey, not the beginning.

Investors must, therefore, adjust their expectations and understand the new metrics in the context of the speed at which companies are being created, growing staff and revenue, and expanding globally. The leverage in the systems from technology and the people web is mesmerizing.

Private Markets Are the New Public Markets, In A Way

Companies that went public during the first decade of the 21st century were six years old on average. By 2015 that average had risen to 10 years old.

Not only are companies remaining private longer. They're also expanding much faster domestically and internationally. That combination means they go public as much more mature companies and at much higher valuations.

Is this good or bad?

From one perspective, we have more mature companies that are less likely to fail.

From another, it means that public shareholders get to hop on the train at a much later stage of the growth cycle. The result is that the appreciation that normally would have happened in the public market is happening in the private market.

Companies go public at much higher valuations now for several fundamental reasons:

- They remained private longer because they have access to capital.
- They raised more money while private.
- Today it takes a lot less money and time to start, sustain, and expand a business.

The cost of building and launching a website went from $5 million to $5,000 in less than 20 years.

Today, there's an internet-connected computer device in everyone's pocket, and we're using them, on average, more than 200 times a day.

The iPhone is more powerful than many desktop computers five years ago. Computers are everywhere. The markets for them are expanding while the cost of attacking those markets is going down. It's a lot cheaper to market a product/service globally, and this is reflected in the valuations of private companies.

It's never been cheaper to start and sustain a business.

You can rent on-demand technology and expertise instead of owning or hiring full-time employees. You can produce on-demand instead of building inventories. You can sell through the internet instead of setting up an expensive brick-and-mortar shop. If you're on the internet, the whole world is your market. Social networks like Facebook and Twitter have changed the way we make purchasing decisions.

Yet it has never been more expensive to become a publicly traded company.

As a result, many new companies remain private longer, raise more money in private markets, and go public at higher price tags. There's much less risk for the public investor with more mature entities. So valuations are, naturally, higher.

It has become harder to get small companies to market. The venture capital industry is playing the role that the public market used to play for micro-cap IPOs. As a result, nearly all of the market value of public technology companies is accruing while they're still private.

The IPO market has changed tremendously over the past few decades. It used to be that companies went public because they needed cash to expand. High-growth companies can now raise all the money they need in private markets. Look at the data in Figure 3-2, and see if you notice a trend.

Figure 3-2

Company	Total Venture Capital Raised (millions)
Microsoft	$1
Apple	$3.6
Intel	$2.5
Cisco Systems	$2.5
Google	$25
Webvan	$441
Facebook	$2,426
Uber	$4,000

Uber went from a $4 million company during its first money raise to a $40 billion company in four years. Uber is an extreme example, but you get the point.

There's plenty of money in private markets. Companies with exciting growth stories can raise all the money they need or want in private markets. When such highly desired companies finally file for an IPO, a limited number of their shares are allocated to select funds. Usually, on their first trading day, such stocks will open substantially above their IPO price.

In other words, ordinary public investors like you and us will get the chance to buy such stocks a lot later in their growth stages at very high valuations.

We're not saying that it's become impossible to make money in popular companies past their IPOs. Facebook is a good recent example of the opposite. We are saying that gone are the days when a well-known market leader will go public and deliver a 10,000% or even a 1,000% return.

Facebook had a rough first six months, but it managed to find new income streams by diversifying its product portfolio and figuring out how to monetize mobile.

Figure 3-3

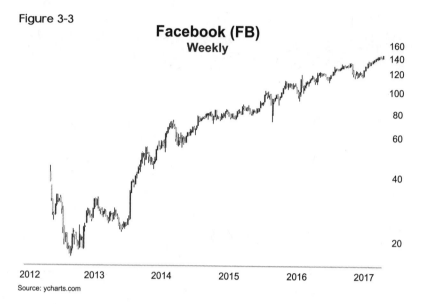

Facebook (FB)
Weekly

Source: ycharts.com

Mark Zuckerberg's social media monster managed to grow its earnings and sales at an impressive manner for several years. Very few companies are able to achieve that performance nowadays, especially if they're so popular.

Take a look at Twitter's venture rounds and the price action after its IPO.

Figure 3-4

Twitter's Venture Rounds and Liquidity Events	Valuation
Series A (2007) – Raised $3 million	$17 million
Series B (2008) – Raised $22 million	$70 million
Series C (2009) – Raised $100 million	$1 billion
2010 – Raised $200 million	$3.7 billion
August 2010 – Raised $800 million	$8 billion
December 2011 – Raised $300 million	$8.4 billion
December 2013 IPO – Raised $2.09 billion	$16 billion
End of first trading day	$24 billion

In early 2017 the market thinks Twitter is worth $11 billion. Maybe it's too early to judge Twitter. But given its current market cap, it would be extremely difficult to see it evolving into the next Microsoft or the next Apple.

We might not see as many 10-baggers in the public market due to major changes in financing and tech infrastructure, but public markets will remain a solid source of liquid opportunities. A lot more value will be created pre-IPO, but public companies with solid growth potential will still enjoy substantial returns.

Why?

Because we're running out of stocks. This is not a joke. In fact it's the law — the law of supply and demand.

In 1976, there were 4,796 listed stocks in the U.S. market. That number spiraled to 7,322 in 1996 in the midst of the dot-com boom. By 2016, there were only 3,671 listed stocks.

Bankruptcies, acquisitions, mergers, and companies staying private longer have shrunk the investible universe in U.S. markets. IPOs might be going public at high valuations, but there are very few of them. A lot of money has to chase only a few high quality new IPOs.

In a bull market, this means that what looks expensive can get a lot more expensive from a short-term perspective.

How to Cope with the Change in Public Markets

If the majority of wealth nowadays is created pre-IPO, is there still a way for public investors to benefit from new listings?

The big money is usually made at extremes that are out of most people's comfort zones. In our eyes, there are two major ways public investors can approach the challenge of ever-changing IPO markets:

- Go after stocks from hated, ignored, or boring industries when they clear new all-time highs from a proper base. In this case, perceptions are worse than reality. Low expectations and new highs create a powerful combination.

- Go after stocks from the hottest industries at the time when they clear new all-time highs from a proper base.

Those two approaches seem diametrically opposed, yet they share something in common: the requirement for a new all-time high.

Why is it so important to wait for a new market issue to build a base and then break out to new all-time highs? Because it's an indication that a company's shares are accumulated by institutions. When institutions buy, they intend to hold for years, so, essentially, they're removing supply from the market.

Now, let's go over each of those approaches and explain why they could provide you with an edge.

Go Where Few Dare Tread

In bull markets most companies go public at very high valuations by default. There are two occasions when valuations might be much more reasonable.

The first is when a company goes public during market correction or after a prolonged period of market decline.

Managed cloud computing company Rackspace went public at the worst possible time in recent financial history — the summer of 2008, when most people wouldn't touch stocks with 20-foot pole.

A rule of thumb says to ignore companies that go public during financial crises because raising money in crappy markets is usually a sign of desperation.

Rackspace was about roughly a $1 billion dollar company on its IPO day in late 2008. In early 2013 it reached $10 billion market cap before it gave up half of it.

The second occasion is when a company belongs to an industry most are afraid of or it's not enticing enough for most people to care.

Vipshop Holdings (VIPS) was one of the only two Chinese companies to get listed in U.S. markets in 2012.

Figure 3-5

Vipshop Holdings (VIPS)
Weekly

VIPS split 10-for-1 in November 2014.

It was a $6 stock when it broke out to
new all-time highs in August 2012.

32.00

16.00

8.00

4.00

2.00

1.00

0.50

0.25

2012   2013   2014   2015

Source: ycharts.com

There were so many frauds related to Chinese stocks in the previous several years that, at the time, most people didn't even consider owning anything Chinese.

Vipshop opened as a $200 million company in March 2012. In February 2015 its market cap approached $15 billion.

When SolarCity completed its IPO in late 2012, the solar sector was one of the most hated and ignored — for good reason. It was down 90% for the previous four years. SolarCity had to slash its IPO offering from a range of $13 to$15 to $8. But by February 2014 it was trading at $88.

Emerge Energy Services sells sand to oil and gas drillers. No one really cared about sand during the raging bull market in 2013. People usually don't care about sand in any market, which means when a sand company goes public, expectations are very low.

Low expectations usually mean low valuation. The only way for a boring business like selling sand to get investors' attention is if it starts to deliver substantial earnings and sales growth.

This is exactly what happened with EMES.

Figure 3-6

Source: ycharts.com

It turned out that fracking (extracting oil and gas through horizontal drilling) requires a lot of sand, and sand companies were making a killing at the time. Emerge Energy went from $17 to $140 in about a year. Then crude oil collapsed and took with it all energy-related stocks.

The lesson? Small float, a few better-than-expected earnings reports, and a hot industry in a bull market can go a long way.

Many of the best-performing IPOs of the past 10 years had an element of surprise in them. They either came from sectors that everyone hated at the time, or they went public when people hated equities in general. In both cases, nobody expected them to perform well, which probably means that their valuations weren't too elevated.

There was one more very important ingredient they shared: They all spent a lot of time on the all-time high list.

Go After the Hottest Industries of the Day

Recent IPOs in a hot industry can move very substantially and very quickly, 50% in a month, 100% in a quarter, several hundred percent in a year. There are always exceptions, but those types of moves are rarely sustained for long.

Between 1999 and 2008, crude oil went from $12 to $147 per barrel. This gigantic appreciation resurrected the clean-tech industry. For a few short years, the solar industry was the king of the market. First Solar went from $30 to $300 in 2007 after it cleared new all-time highs from a small IPO base. Then it dropped all the way down to $11 by mid-2012.

3D printing stocks were on fire in 2012 and 2013. 3D Systems went up from $10 to $100 in two years. Such profits inspire and capture the imagination of the crowd. Such quick price appreciation is accepted as validation that all the stories about the potential of 3D printing will become a reality, which leads to a huge spike in demand for 3D printing stocks.

No worries. The Wall Street printing and marketing machine is always here to oblige.

If you're a company operating in a hot industry, the odds are that someone will call you and pitch the opportunity to go public right here, right now. This is how many industry trends end — by over-satiating demand.

A couple new 3D stocks debuted on public markets in early 2013 — ExOne went from $25 to $80 in six months. By early 2015 it was trading around $15. Voxeljet went from $20 to $79 in five weeks. By early 2015 it was trading around $9 per share.

Figure 3-7

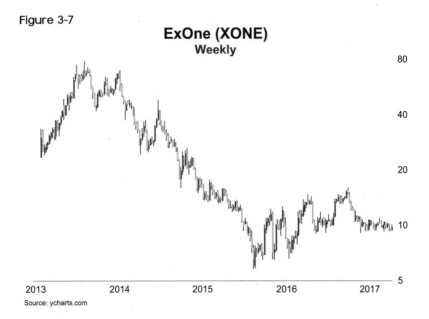

ExOne (XONE)
Weekly

Source: ycharts.com

The lesson? Don't overstay your welcome in recent IPOs that be-long to a hot industry. Most of them will turn out to be short-term fads and will end up trading significantly below their IPO prices.

The same process happened in biotech stocks in 2013 and 2014. Several dozen stocks went up between 50% and 500% in a very short period of time. The majority of them gave back up most of their profits within a year. The same patterns repeat over and over again because the incentives and the psychology of the key decision-makers haven't changed.

The proper timing of an IPO makes all the difference in the world. A bull market can be very generous and forgive all sins of speculators. All news is good news in a bull market. All news is bad news in a bear market.

In 2014, any biotech IPO was eagerly awaited and generously re-warded. Calithera Biosciences and Coherus BioSciences went from $10 to $30 in the first three months after their IPOs. Atara Biotherapeutics went from $10 to $40 in six months. Cellular Biomedicine went from $5 to $40 in nine months.

Figure 3-8

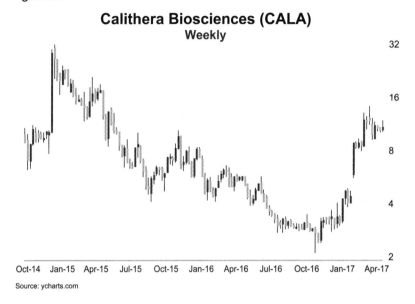

Calithera Biosciences (CALA)
Weekly

Source: ycharts.com

Figure 3-9

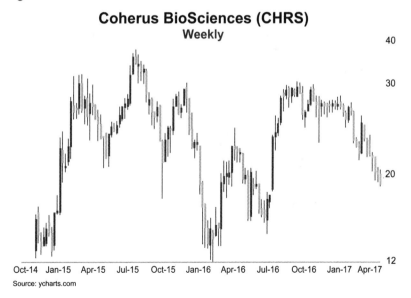

Coherus BioSciences (CHRS)
Weekly

Source: ycharts.com

Figure 3-10

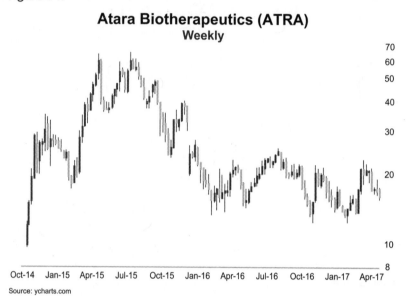

Atara Biotherapeutics (ATRA)
Weekly

Source: ycharts.com

These are just a few examples of the crazy momentum that developed in the biotech space.

Don't Overstay Your Welcome

If recent IPOs belong to a currently hot industry or it's a company that's very popular on its own, the odds are that they went public at extremely high valuations.

A quick and powerful rally after the IPOs has made them even more expensive — expectations are so high that it's pretty much impossible to meet in short-term perspective. Plus, financial markets are quite myopic. They're forward-looking, but they don't look too far into the future.

Recent IPOs are very vulnerable to mean-reversion after their initial rally, for several reasons.

First, supply grows due to secondary offerings, lockup expiration, and new IPOs in the same industry. It's perfectly appropriate for many of the new stocks that go up substantially in a short period of time to issue secondary offerings and dilute current shareholders.

Wall Street is a printing press and a marketing machine. It carefully gauges the health of the market and the current appetite for certain industries. At the end of the day, it offers what the market desires. Supply is unlimited.

Second, companies don't live up to expectations and fail to generate the anticipated earnings and sales growth.

And, third, enthusiasm eventually fades. People wake up. The fear of losing overtakes the fear of missing out. The fear of holding the bag trumps performance-chasing and greed.

The vast majority of IPOs will go through a boom-and-bust process in a short period of time; therefore, the majority of them should be treated as short-term trading vehicles.

Some of them will turn out to be big long-term winners, but you'll have plenty of time to participate in their trends. There's no reason to hurry and buy them on their first trading day.

Due to a small float, it's not unusual to see a recent IPO run 100% or 200% in the first six months of its publicly traded existence and then crash 80% to 90%.

Twitter almost doubled in the first three months after it went public. Then it crashed 80% over the next three years.

Figure 3-11

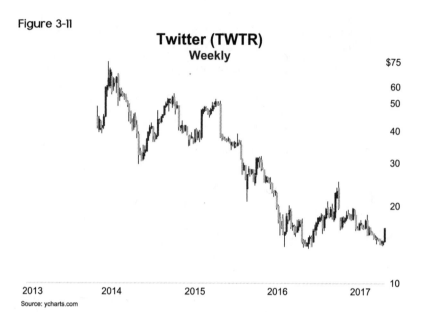

Shake Shack went from $40 to $100 in its first five months. Then it returned to $30 in the next couple of years.

Figure 3-12

Acacia Communications went from $30 to $120 in its first four months. Then it declined 50% in the next five months.

Figure 3-13

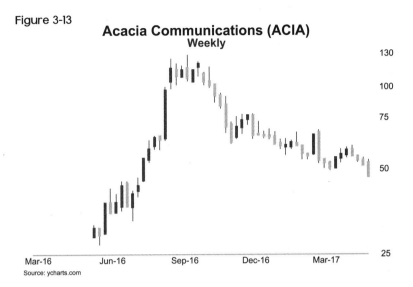

Source: ycharts.com

GoPro skyrocketed from $30 to $100 in its first four months. Then it collapsed 90% in the next three years.

Figure 3-14

Source: ycharts.com

Fitbit went from $30 to $50 in its first two months. Then it collapsed to $5 in the next two years.

Figure 3-15

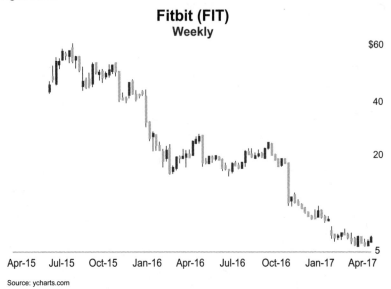

Fitbit (FIT)
Weekly

Source: ycharts.com

The Perfect Trading Vehicle

Recent IPOs can be among the most lucrative trading vehicles in bull markets. If you would like to find stocks that have the potential to run 20% to 50% in one to four weeks, keep a watch list of recent IPOs with tight bases.

If you constantly study the stocks that gain more than 30% in a month, you'll find many recent IPOs among them. There's a reason behind it. They have a lot going for them in a bull market, including institutional support.

Meanwhile, insiders are locked up and can't sell for six to 12 months following the IPO. And, finally, float is small, so even a slight uptick in demand is enough to send shares much higher in a very short period.

If you want to understand why IPOs are among the best short-term trading vehicles, you need to educate yourself on the concept of float and what it means for supply-and-demand dynamics. Float is the actual number of shares available to the general public. Here's the equation:

- Float = Shares Outstanding — Restricted shares

The number of outstanding shares is voted by the board of directors of each company.

Restricted shares are owned by insiders, a group that includes founders, management, employees, and venture capitalists.

Companies always sell a minority stake during their IPOs. You'll notice that most newly public companies' float is only 10% to 20% of their total shares outstanding.

The rest are restricted shares, owned by insiders who aren't allowed to sell for the six to 12 months following the IPO. This restriction isn't due to Securities and Exchange Commission regulations. It's a function of underwriting investment banks' desire to create a favorable market for new issues.

Google floated less than 20 million shares for its IPO in 2004. The rest became available six months after the IPO. Google — now known as Alphabet — has a float of approximately 600 million shares. In other words, it takes a lot more buying and selling power to move this ship.

Microsoft's float was only 20 million shares in 1986. Now it's 7.6 billion shares.

Twitter IPO'd with 70 million shares out of 615 million shares outstanding.

Small float, a bull market, and a good story are an explosive catalytic combination. When thousands of institutions compete to own a small number of stocks, we could see gigantic moves in short periods of time.

A low float is a double-edged sword. It leads to huge drawdowns during market corrections. It's not unusual for a recent IPO to go down 50% to 80% when the S&P 500 corrects 10% to 15%. Such big selloffs create incredible buying opportunities, because valuations drop to extremely low levels. When the stock market bounces back, their recovery is often as quick and furious as their decline.

Recent IPOs deliver incredible profits after a market correction is over. And by incredible, we mean 100% to 200% in three to 12 weeks.

Let's review the correction in early 2016 to illustrate our point.

From January 1, 2016, to mid-February 2016, the S&P 500 declined 8%. There were no IPOs in January. In February there were five. Only three companies went public in December 2015, and they all got hit pretty hard during the market correction from January to early February.

Yirendai was one of them. Its initial float was 7.5 million shares out of 59 million outstanding shares. Yirendai was absolutely decimated during the market correction in January. It went from $10 to under $3.50 a share in early February.

Figure 3-16

Yirendai (YRD)
Weekly

Source: ycharts.com

Guess what happened after the market started to recover in mid-February. By April 2016 it was trading near $14. By August it was trading near $40 per share.

Those low-floaters can move a lot, in both directions.

Ivaylo elaborates on how to trade recent IPOs in his books *The 5 Secrets To Highly Profitable Swing Trading* and *Top 10 Trading Setups: How to Find Them, When to Trade Them, How to Make Money with Them*.

Check them out if you're interested in short-term market speculation.

FOUR

Is Investing In What You Love and Know A Good Idea?

"Common sense is not so common."

— Voltaire

"Not everything that can be counted counts and not everything that counts can be counted."

— Albert Einstein

Not So Secret

There are two basic ways to come up with great investment ideas.

The first way is to start with price. This approach will generate ideas in areas you don't necessarily understand. But you don't have to know all there is to know about a company or industry in order to make money. At the very least, you could quickly educate yourself.

There's always a simple explanation behind every move. Sometimes it's worth it to just close your eyes and follow price. We elaborate on this approach in Chapter Five.

The second way is to start with something you love or you have noticed that other people are going crazy about and then confirm whether the market agrees with your feeling or the consensus around you.

Seeing your stocks on the 52-week high list is the market's way of agreeing with consumers.

The second approach was at the cornerstone for one of the best-performing mutual fund managers in U.S. financial history, Peter Lynch.

Between 1977 and 1990, Lynch produced a compounded average annual return of 29%, generating a total gain of 2,700% for his investors. During the same timeframe the S&P 500 appreciated 200%.

Peter Lynch retired in 1990, but he remains the mutual fund manager with the best track record ever. His "secret": Buy what you know.

The Best Ideas Will Find You

How could your passion for a product or a service make you a lot of money?

Everyone has a passion for something. Everyone is an expert in a certain area. Some enjoy building rockets. Some love shopping. Some like eating out.

How many have ever tried to really make money out of their passions?

They say that if you love what you do, you'll be tremendously successful. The big question is, could you be tremendously successful if you invest in what you love?

Yes, you could.

Warren Buffett said it best:

People are going to get out of bed and work productively around the world to meet the needs of their family. People are going to spend and there will always be some companies that will sell something that people would love to trade their money against.

Everyone shops, eats, wears clothes. Our consumer habits could be an excellent source of incredible investment ideas.

Products and brands come into and go out of fashion. Many consumer trends last only a few years. But they could deliver 1,000% returns before they end.

Don't be afraid to invest in places where you and your friends love to eat. Every decade gives us restaurant chains that transform many investors' lives.

Chipotle Mexican Grill went up 1,500% in its first nine years as a public company.

Figure 4-1

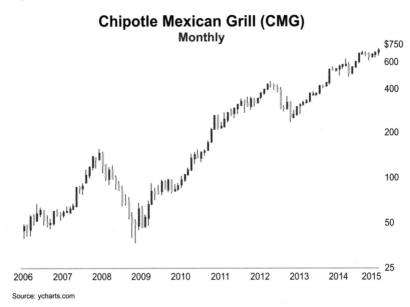

Chipotle Mexican Grill (CMG)
Monthly

Source: ycharts.com

Domino's Pizza went from $10 to $100 between 2010 and 2014.

Figure 4-2

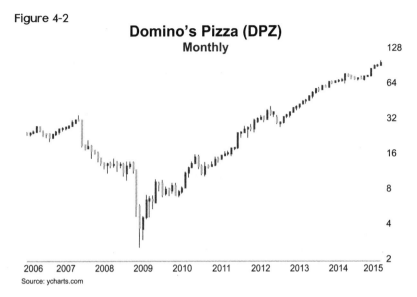

Buffalo Wild Wings is up 1,600% since its IPO in late 2003.

Figure 4-3

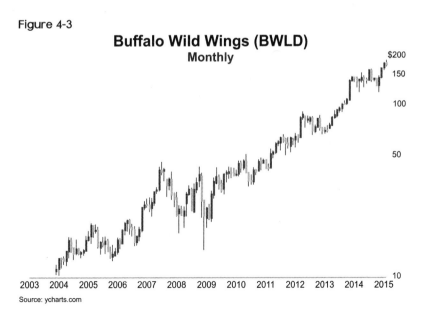

Some trends just hit you over the head. In 2006 you could see Ugg boots on every street in America. The stock of Ugg's Australia-based maker, Deckers Outdoor, went up 1,000% between 2006 and 2011.

Figure 4-4

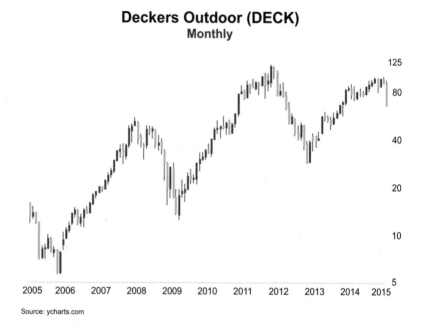

Deckers Outdoor (DECK)
Monthly

Source: ycharts.com

People vote with their dollars every day. So does Wall Street.

Fashion constantly changes and brings new names on the scene. At least a couple years before Michael Kors went public in December 2011 every woman knew it was the latest hot brand to own. Its stock went from $25 to $100 in the two years following its IPO.

Figure 4-5

Michael Kors Holdings (KORS)
Monthly

Source: ycharts.com

By 2010 yoga had fully seeped into the popular consciousness. Many of us bought $100 pants from Lululemon. But how many of us decided to invest in its stock? Lululemon went from $3 to $80 between 2009 and 2012.

Figure 4-6

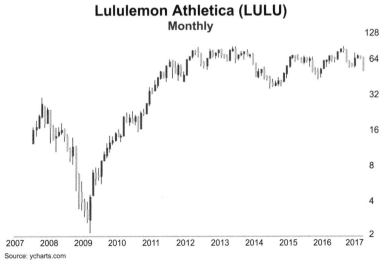

Lululemon Athletica (LULU)
Monthly

Source: ycharts.com

You likely noticed that you and your friends or your kids went crazy about energy drinks in 2003. If you happened to check the stocks
of the products you were buying, you would have noticed that a small
company now known as Monster Beverage but then called Hansen
Natural was pushing out to new multiyear highs.

Figure 4-7

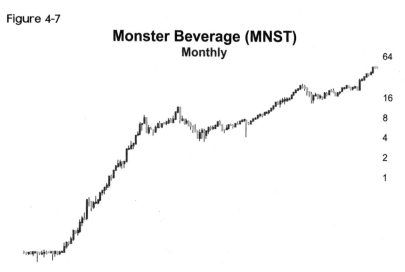

Monster Beverage (MNST)

Source: ycharts.com

That translated into huge gains for early investors: $5,000 invested
in Monster Beverage in 2003 was worth about $2.3 million in early
2015.

Not too bad for a sugary drink with a lot of caffeine.

Here's Howard describing how he found and approached investing in two of the biggest trends of the past decade, Chipotle Mexican
Grill and Apple.

Howard on Chipotle:

*Six or eight months after I had been eating at Chipotle once a week with my
daughter, I heard that they were doing an IPO. I wrote about it, saying, "It
doesn't matter what happens with this IPO. Whatever price it comes out at, it*

is a buy." I was confident after eating there all that time and seeing how they ran the restaurant, how four people could run an operation like that, and how simple the menu was. They also did the little things that made eating there a great experience. It was not like a usual fast-food restaurant, but the prices were pretty much the same.

What excited me most was they were in only a few South-western states, so they had a lot of opportunity in front of them. America had 300 million people. When you find a chain that is run the way Chipotle is, and then you see that it is in only a few states, you feel like you really have something. The really nice thing is that Chipotle is a cookie-cutter operation, meaning that they figured out how to run it, so it was just a matter of duplicating the formula. I believed it was a trend I could jump on. When your kid likes it and you like it too, it is an easy decision. You just know that you are going to make money with something like that. When you have that confidence, you can tune out a lot of the noise. When Chipotle came public, I bought it. The stock nearly tripled in eight months.

Howard on Apple:

My encounter with the iPod in 2005 is another good example of how I did some groundwork and experienced the product. I have never been comfortable with gadgets, but the iPod resonated with me the first time I picked one up. Then when I went to work out at the health club I would see a few people wearing those white iPod ear buds and I know in my heart that within a year or two, nine out of ten people will have those ear buds. I would not buy the stock because it was not even close to being at an all-time high; buying it then would have violated my boundaries.

But I did buy an iPod and I was using it, and it just so happened that an Apple store stood across the street from my office. I found myself in that store all the time and I noticed how busy it was and how much activity there was around the product. Eventually the stock started to moving up and the stronger it got, the more confident I became. I did not buy it at $12 a share, the approximate price at the time. I waited until the stock tripled (still not all-time high) and by then it has risen to about $40 (pre-splits). I could not resist. I felt it in my bones.

Sure enough, the white ear buds were all over the health club and the stock went up over 400% in the next two years. The iPod was a product I used and liked. It came from a place where I shop and was part of the lifestyle that I have adopted. The people around me also used it and liked it. All of those things gave me comfort in the catalyst for the stock. I could shut out the naysayers. I was actually emboldened by them, as they would be fuel for the fire when they finally purchased an Apple product. My investing standpoint was not all that different from my consumer stand point — I was part of the trend. I was not the first person to buy an iPod or Apple stock, but that didn't mean I couldn't make money.

Howard elaborates on his social approach to investing in his first book, *The WallStrip Edge: Using Trends to Make Money — Find Them, Ride Them, and Get Off.*

The lesson? If you love a certain product or service and use it every day, if it makes your life better, the odds are that there are a lot more people that feel the same about it.

We're much more alike than we think. We're wired to react similarly in the same situations and circumstances. Use that to your advantage. Think like an investor. Make the connection between a great product or service and the respective company's stock.

Learn how to make money out of your own shopping habits, out of your friend's shopping habits.

If investing in what you love has been shown to be so simple and profitable, why are more people not doing it?

Exactly.

We've asked ourselves the same question year after year as we've seen trend after trend. Most people simply don't think that way. Very few are making the connection between a product they love and the stock of the company that makes that product.

Most people just invest in mutual funds and ETFs. They don't even think about individual companies.

You could own part of someone else's business. You might not have a say in what should happen, but you could participate in the growth of a hot brand as an investor.

You could go to dinner at your favorite diner and make a lot of money while it's expanding.

You could wear your favorite shoes and make a lot of money as their sales grow around the world and new outlets pop up everywhere.

They say that the best investment you could make is in your own business. But, in reality, you often have a much bigger chance of succeeding by investing in an already profitable, growing business as a public shareholder.

Yes, it's true that you're getting the worst-possible paper a company could issue — common stock.

But it's also true that you could make a lot of money doing it.

Quantifying Social Trends

You could connect the dots between your own, your family's, and your friends' consumer habits and investing opportunities. Or you could use a more scientific approach.

Big data has revolutionized decision-making in many industries, including investing.

LikeFolio is a website that helps the discovery process of hot consumer trends by scanning social media. It reveals in real time what brands, products, and services are getting more or less popular, and it quantifies people's sentiment toward them. Its sentiment data combined with a proper price filter could be a powerful idea generation tool.

Here's fintech entrepreneur Andy Swan explaining how Tesla popped early on LikeFolio's radar:

When a company's primary product starts getting mentioned 20, 50, 100 times as often as it did just a short time ago…. there might be something significant going on.

Such was the case with Tesla a few years back.

People talked about Tesla 140 times as much at the end of 2012 (almost all positive) as they did at the beginning of 2012. 140 times!

When you combine this social signal with a breakout to new 52-week highs from a long technical base, you get a powerful investment idea.

A Company and Its Stock Aren't the Same Thing

Let's assume you love a certain product and you use it every day. You buy the stock on that basis. What do you do next?

Do you just hold for years and wait for business growth to manifest via stock appreciation? What if everyone else has already noticed the same trend and has also scooped up shares?

Investing is not about just buying a piece of a business. It's about understanding how catalysts will change people's perceptions over time.

Catalysts include earnings and sales growth, valuation, price momentum, market sentiment, competition, new products and/or services, management, and new regulations.

Just because a product is popular doesn't mean the stock of the company that produces it will make you rich.

You might be too early or too late as an investor. It's not an exception to see price trends end before earnings and sales growth slow down. You could lose a lot of money, or you could gain very little, if you buy a great business at the wrong time.

Proper timing of your purchase is not just essential. It's everything.

The same Lululemon that went from $3 to $80 between 2009 and 2012 had a 50% correction in 2013-14. The same Michael Kors that went from $25 to $100 between 2012 and early 2014 had a 40% correction over the ensuing 12 months. The same Netflix that went from $30 to $300 from 2009 to mid-2011 had an 80% decline in the five months after that.

The lesson? The stocks of products and services that you continue to love and use could have substantial corrections. Investing in what you love is a double-edged sword.

The outcome of your investment depends on the price you pay for it and on the price other people are willing to pay for it in the future.

When you buy a stock, you aren't buying a piece of business. You're buying the current expectations about the future of this business. Sometimes it pays to buy extremely low expectations — the value investor's approach. Other times, it pays to buy rising expectations — the momentum investor's approach.

There could be a huge disconnect between the stock market, which is forward-looking, and people's passions, which exist in the present.

We find it useful to combine the "invest in what you know" approach with the 52-week high list to make sure that social momentum has materialized in price momentum.

Remember, we can't make a cent before the market agrees with our investment thesis. The market's way of agreeing with us is by sending our stocks to new 52-week highs from a proper technical base.

Early Adopters, Domain Experience, and Investing

The easiest — and often the most reliable — ways to see the future and catch trends are pretty straightforward.

First, look at the 52-week high list. It's often a shortcut to the minds of smart investors.

It could also be a reflection of people's ignorance and stupidity. It takes some practice to learn how to use it properly.

Second, follow the thoughts of people with domain experience — angel investors, early adopters, engineers, specialists, venture capitalists, opinion-leaders.

You don't need to know any people with domain experience personally in order to benefit from their wisdom as an investor. The beauty of the internet and social media is that anyone has access to everyone's brain for a marginal cost.

If you learn how use both tools, you're likely to catch quite a few of the biggest stock market winners.

The good news is that you don't have to be first to recognize a new trend. The trick is to jump when it matters — when price, liquidity, and fear of missing out start to drive investor behavior. It's extremely useful to follow and listen to early adopters in situations where financials alone might cause you to dismiss a great company.

Internet entrepreneur and investor Chris Dixon posted one of the smartest commentaries on the current era for his now-suspended blog in March 2013.

The post, headlined "What the smartest people do on the weekend is what everyone else will do during the week in ten years," crystalized idea generation in the 21st century.

Chris wrote:

Business people vote with their dollars, and are mostly trying to create near-term financial returns. Engineers vote with their time, and are mostly trying to invent interesting new things. Hobbies are what the smartest people spend their time on when they aren't constrained by near-term financial goals.

Talking to smart people who are considered experts in their respective fields could give you a profound insight into future trends. But how actionable is the information you receive from them?

We have to be careful how we consume information. Everything we do, everything we read and watch impacts our decision-making, consciously or subconsciously. Talking to people who are perceived as experts in their fields doesn't always produce positive results.

In April 2012 Howard wrote a blog post to explain how he was convinced by a bunch of smart people to sell his Netflix position just before it quadrupled. It's a good lesson for all aspiring investors:

I have no position in Netflix. I put one in December (on the Stocktwits stream) when the stock was in the 90 $ and went to hang with some very smart people who had me convinced the Disney Deal was going to kill them. I let outside opinions influence (people I trusted that were super smart) the price and catalysts that were the reason for my investment in the first place. Now the stock has doubled. The catalyst may or may not be fully priced in, but Netflix is dominating on engagement and eyeballs.

Netflix is now trading near $1,000 per share (adjusted for a 7-for-1 stock split completed in 2015). This is a typical example of how knowing too much and trusting perceived experts could hurt you.

Figure 4-8

Netflix (NFLX)
Monthly

Source: ycharts.com

There's a saying on Wall Street: If you don't know why you're in a stock, then you won't know when to exit. Translated for Main Street, that means, in most cases, you'll exit at some random point that doesn't maximize the potential of your investment.

From another side, we know people who were bullish on Tesla months before the electric carmaker started to appear in the mainstream press and well before people started to rave about its stock.

Here's a screenshot of an email conversation Ivan had in September 2012 with Dustin Schneider, who was one of StockTwits' leading engineers at the time:

Dustin Schneider <dustin@stocktwits.com>   **9/10/12** ☆

to me ▾

I like TSLA for 2 main reasons:

1) Elon Musk.
2) Heavy R&D and in-house manufacturing.

It may not be a good stock but it's a good company doing serious engineering
led by one of the best visionaries of our generation. That's my two cents
whether you want it or not.

[•••]

Ivanhoff <ivanhoff@stocktwits.com>   **9/10/12** ☆ ↰ ▾

to Dustin ▾

Long-term, they seem to be the major player in the industry. Market is always
short-sighted and doesn't look beyond 6 to 12 months which is a good thing
for smart, patient investors, but you also need people with capital power
(funds) to agree with you and buy the stock in order to make money.

[•••]

You didn't have to buy Tesla in September 2012 to make money.
If you did, your capital was allocated to an asset that went nowhere for
six months. You could have waited for it to report better-than-expected
earnings and gap to new all-time highs near $40 in April 2013.

Figure 4-9

Tesla Motors (TSLA)
Monthly

You would still have enjoyed most of the move afterward. Tesla reached an all-time high of $291 in September 2014.

Passive and Active Catalysts

Passive catalysts are value and the opinion of smart people with domain experience. They don't tell you when to buy or sell. They do tell you how far a move could go once an active catalyst is presented. And there's only one actionable catalyst that matters: liquidity.

In other words, only price pays.

Listening to geeks — engineers, industry experts, marketing gurus, experienced angel investors and venture capitalists, insightful visionaries and futurists — is always smart. They see and talk about future big trends before anyone else.

Blindly acting on their recommendations in the stock market is a whole different game, though. It doesn't matter how smart you are or how incredibly ingenious your investment thesis sounds. Unless and until the market agrees with you, you won't make a cent. The beauty of the stock market is that you don't need to be first or original in order to make money.

People with domain experience can see trends long before anyone else. This could be a huge advantage if it's juxtaposed with an understanding of price — and that means the ability to read charts. If price is not added as an additional filter, three things are possible.

Experts could enter very early and put money to work in a non-performing asset. It won't start making any money before the market starts to agree with you. It might take months. It might take years. It might not happen at all.

They could, alternatively, stay too long and see their gains disappear. If you were a big believer in the potential of 3D printing stocks in early 2012, you made a lot of money. 3D Systems went up 1,000% between early 2012 and late 2013. If you decided to hold your 3D stocks longer in anticipation of even bigger profits, you would've seen a 70% drawdown in the next year.

They also might see threats where they don't matter and exit trends way too early because of their deep understanding of a particular industry. They could be in too early and out too early and miss out on most of the gains. Comparatively, guys who rely primarily on price could catch the meatiest part of a trend without knowing much about an industry or the catalysts.

Why Even Bother?

If noticing a popular product or service is not enough to buy the stocks behind them, why do we even bother? Why don't we just pay attention to the 52-week high list and choose our investments from there purely based on price action?

What's the purpose behind investing in something you understand?

You might notice a trend before Wall Street. You don't want to be too early because your capital might be stuck in a non-productive asset that doesn't generate any return. You don't want to be too late, either, and put money to work after major media outlets start to feature your stocks of interest in their primetime slots or on their front pages.

If you understand the catalysts, you're less likely to be shaken out by normal price pullbacks. You also won't pay attention to scary headlines with the singular goal of attracting more page views.

You're a consumer by default — we all are. We shop. We dine. How hard would it be to learn to connect products and services you love with their stocks? This approach has a proven record of great success.

Then there's the question about further shrinking the universe of stocks you could invest in. In any given year, there could be thousands of stocks showing up on the 52-week high list.

You can't possibly own all of them. One way to capture big potential winners is to focus on trends, where you also participate as a consumer. Understanding the story behind a move is one very smart way to filter and limit the universe of stocks you're interested in.

There's also the question of asset allocation. Understanding the catalysts behind a price move justifies using a bigger position size compared to situations where price is the only reason you get involved.

Investing in what you love is not a flawless approach. There's always a danger that your love for a product could turn you into a biased investor with clouded judgment. Never love anything that can't love you back.

The market doesn't love anyone. It doesn't care about your personal agenda. Understanding the catalyst behind a price move could be extremely useful, but it's never enough on its own.

Price action, on the other hand, could be a beginning and an end to your market approach on its own.

FIVE

Does Past Performance Impact Future Returns?

"The obvious rarely happens, the unexpected constantly occurs."

— Irish proverb

"Sometimes being a contrarian means staying with the trend."

— Steven Spencer

Price Is Right

We all feel more comfortable investing in businesses we understand, in products we can touch, in services we can experience.

The big question is whether we're missing some incredible opportunities by focusing only on what we understand and can explain.

It doesn't matter how smart you think you are or how innovative your investment idea is. Unless and until the market agrees with you, you won't make a cent.

The market's way of agreeing with you is by sending your long ideas to the new 52-week high list and even the all-time high list.

Since price is the only thing that pays, doesn't it make sense to rely on price action only for our buy and sell decisions?

Past Performance Could Be a Powerful Stock-Selection Tool

Past performance is not a guarantee for future returns. That's the most standard Wall Street disclosure. Nothing is guaranteed to anyone. No stock-picking criterion is flawless and works all the time.

And yet, every year, like clockwork, the same patterns repeat, over and over again.

The beauty of financial markets is that you don't have to be first in order to profit from a trend. No one knows which new all-time high is the beginning or an end of a journey. No one knows how far a trend could go or how long it could last.

Monster Beverage hit new 52-week highs in July 2003, and it kept going higher. Three years after its breakout, it traded 9,000% higher.

Figure 5-1

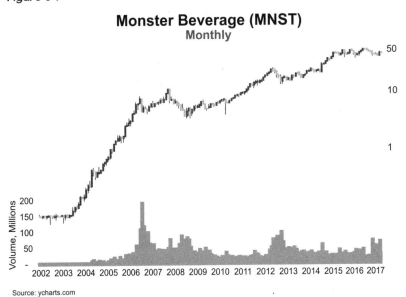

Source: ycharts.com

Amazon cleared new all-time highs in October 2009 from a long base. It went up 800% in the next seven years.

Figure 5-2

Ambarella broke out to new all-time highs in October 2013 near $20 per share. Less than two years later, it was trading near $130.

Figure 5-3

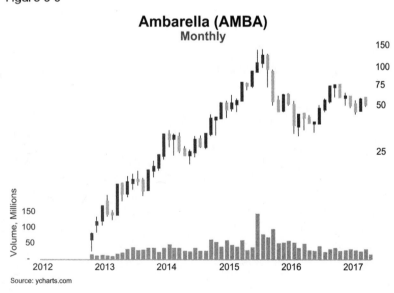

Past performance could be an incredible source of investing ideas. By past performance, we mean two things, momentum and new 52-week highs.

Stocks that outperformed in the past three to 12 months tend to continue to outperform in the next three to 12 months. That's momentum

The father of value investing, Benjamin Graham, says that when people are shopping for common stocks, they should choose them the way they buy groceries, not the way they buy perfume. It's true that perfumes go in and out of favor and could be significantly overpriced, but no trend lasts forever, not in the market or in real life.

There are trends that continue for only three months; there are trends that continue for three years. Each could be a source of substantial profits for an investor with basic risk-management skills. "Popular and overvalued" is very different from "going down tomorrow."

You could never truly know where in a trend you are buying. Stocks could go up 100% in six months and then keep going higher for a lot longer.

All long-term stock market winners spend a considerable time on the 52-week high list, if not the all-time high list. It helps you identify great investment ideas about which you know very little but you could easily educate yourself.

You don't need to be an expert in a field in order to invest in it and, most importantly, make money.

Momentum Works

There is no free lunch.

Howard Marks, the founder of Oaktree Capital Group, has said that great performance today often takes away from future performance. It's like spending borrowed money: You will have to pay it back in the future, which will decrease your spending power.

Marks is right. The stock market is often forward-looking. Sometimes it will even go insane and price a future that seems completely unattainable at the moment. The market could discount the next 20 years' worth of potential earnings, inside 12 months. The stock market constantly overreacts. A stock could go up from $20 to $200 in a year without having a single profitable quarter and then go sideways for 10 years or decline as the underlying company starts to actually earn money.

The good news is that we can participate in a trend on the way up and not give back most of our profits when that trend inevitably ends.

The Next Big Thing Is Often the Last Big Thing

People too often ask what the next big thing is. Sometimes the next big thing is the last big thing. Some trends last a lot longer than anyone could expect, comprehend, or imagine.

Strong stocks leave traces, so you could participate in part of their trends. Take, for example, Pharmacyclics. It doubled in 2011, quadrupled in 2012, doubled again in 2013, and basically finished flat in 2014, only to double again in the first three months of 2015, when it was acquired. During that time, it set up multiple technical bases, and it broke out to new all-time highs hundreds of times. You didn't need a time machine or inside information or expert knowledge on biotech to notice this trend.

Price momentum was all you needed to spot and participate in this monstrous trend.

Coherent went up 120% in 2016. Then it appreciated another 50% in the first quarter of 2017.

Figure 5-4

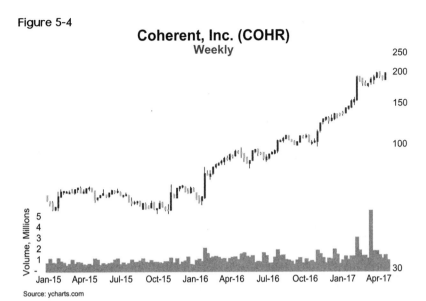

Coherent, Inc. (COHR)
Weekly

Source: ycharts.com

Advanced Micro Devices doubled from February 2016 to May 2016. Then it went up another 300% in the next year.

Figure 5-5

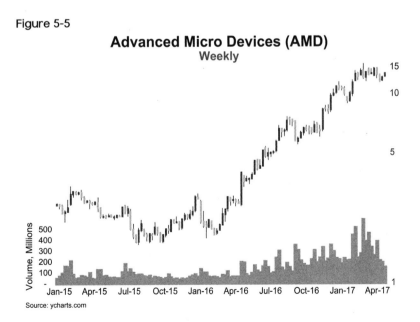

Advanced Micro Devices (AMD)
Weekly

Source: ycharts.com

NVIDIA doubled from September 2016 to May 2016. Then it proceeded to triple on top of that in the next nine months.

Figure 5-6

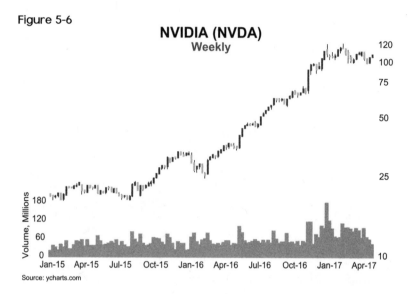

Applied Optoelectronics doubled from June 2016 until September 2016. Then it tripled in the next six months.

Figure 5-7

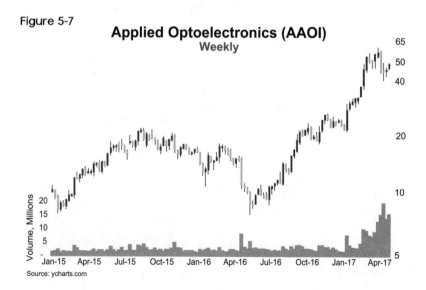

We could train ourselves to recognize good risk/reward setups, but we never know in advance how far a stock could travel. In his book *One Up on Wall Street*, Peter Lynch wrote something similar about his biggest gainers:

> *Frankly, I've never been able to predict which stocks will go up tenfold, or which will go up fivefold. I try to stick with them as long as the story's intact, hoping to be pleasantly surprised. The success of a company isn't the surprise, but what the shares bring often is.*

Prices Change When Expectations Change

In his deeply philosophical book *The Most Important Thing: Uncommon Sense for the Thoughtful Investor*, Howard Marks shares the three stages of a bull market:

- *A few forward-looking people begin to believe that things will get better.*
- *Most investors realize improvement is taking place.*
- *Everyone concludes that things will get better forever.*

This is an excellent description of the sentiment stages of the majority of the big market winners.

The stock market is often forward-looking. A stock could move to a new 52-week high long before its move is confirmed by fundamentals.

When a stock has been trading between $10 and $12 for, let's say, six months and it suddenly starts to change hands above $12, it's usually a sign that something major has changed, either in the fundamentals of the underlying company or in the sentiment of investors.

Someone is willing to pay a price that no one else paid for a long time. Prices don't move out of a long-term range unless investors' and speculators' expectations have changed.

What could be the reason for such a change? Does the reason really matter? Isn't the result more important than its cause?

The reason behind the change in expectations isn't always important. It might be justified for some and not for others. In fact, for most people, the reason is irrelevant. As our friend and seasoned trader Brian Shannon likes to remind us, "Price is the only thing that pays."

Someone might know something that most don't. By following price, you could become his or her silent "partner" and profit from his or her insights, reflected in price action. That person's knowledge could be based on insider information, or it could be based on experience.

The only reason we perceive the same situation differently is because we have had different experiences under similar circumstances or no experience at all. Maybe someone who has lived and traded through enough market cycles sees something that the majority doesn't and starts to buy before fundamentals improve or news is released.

The stock market is forward-looking. Prices don't change when fundamentals change. Prices change when expectations change, and the latter could change for various irrational reasons.

By the time expectations are confirmed or disconfirmed by facts, most of the move might be already over. This is how financial markets often work. They are forward-looking. They price a future that hasn't happened yet. And they'll sometimes price events that might never happen.

The beauty of the market is that your broker doesn't care if you made your money in a trend that was justified by actual improvement in earnings growth or in a trend that was based on sheer speculation.

A stock could go up 100% in six months without the slightest change in fundamentals. Everyone could participate in part of this trend without knowing anything about this stock. The money made or lost in trends we understand and the money made or lost in trends we don't understand have an equal weight.

Only price pays, indeed.

Sometimes, Being a Contrarian Means Staying with the Trend

Twenty-nine stocks went up more than 1,000% in the decade from February 2007 to February 2017. One of them is an airline. Going to Hawaii has clearly been really popular. Seven of the top 10 performers are internet stocks. The other three are biotech companies. It was the decade of the internet and drugs.

What do all of the above stocks have in common, other than being able to grow their earnings and sales in an impressive manner for multiple years? Two things:

- They spent a lot of time on the 52-week high list and set up multiple times.

- Every stock that goes on to make 1,000% first passes the 100% mark along the way.

If you screen for stocks that are already up more than 100% from their 52-week lows, you'll end up with a universe of stocks that contains many future big winners. Granted, some of the stocks on this screen will end up crashing spectacularly, but this is an issue a good risk exit strategy can fix.

The goal of investing is to make a lot of money when you are right and to lose a small amount when you are wrong. Being wrong is often not a choice, but staying wrong always is.

Here are the top 10 performers of the past 10 years.

Figure 5-8

Symbol	Company	10-Year % Change	Last Price	10-Year Low
NFLX	Netflix	4,370%	$143.86	$2.23
PCLN	Priceline	3,052%	$1,651.74	$45.15
AMZN	Amazon.com	2,086%	$855.61	$34.68
EBIX	Ebix	1,803%	$59.20	$2.68
INCY	Incyte	1,793%	$121.36	$1.85
REGN	Regeneron Pharma	1,766%	$370.22	$11.81
BIDU	Baidu	1,643%	$186.01	$9.28
BOFI	Bofl Holding	1,541%	$30.28	$0.75
AXGN	Axogen	1,515%	$10.50	$0.55
NTES	NetEase	1,391%	$304.07	$13.45

And here are the 10-year charts for those top performers, in order.

Figure 5-9

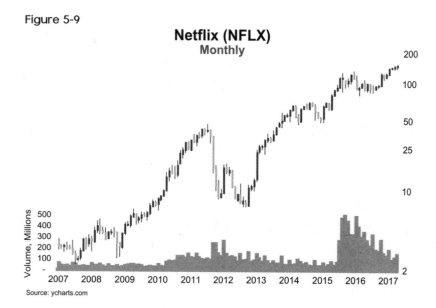

Figure 5-10

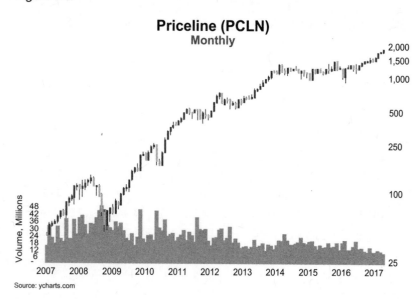

Figure 5-11

Source: ycharts.com

Figure 5-12

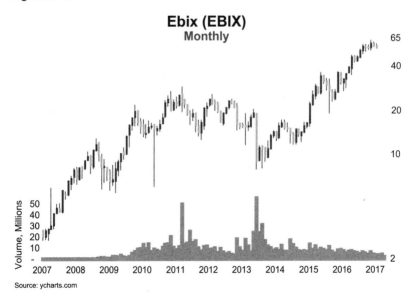

Source: ycharts.com

Figure 5-13

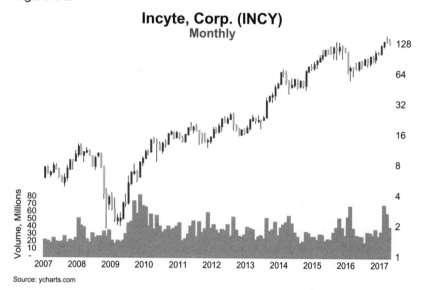

Source: ycharts.com

Figure 5-14

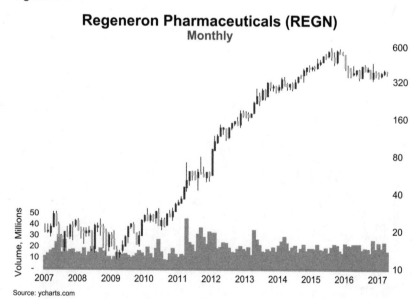

Source: ycharts.com

Figure 5-15

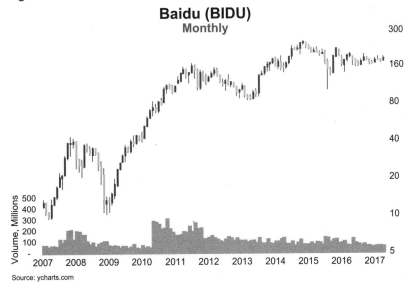

Source: ycharts.com

Figure 5-16

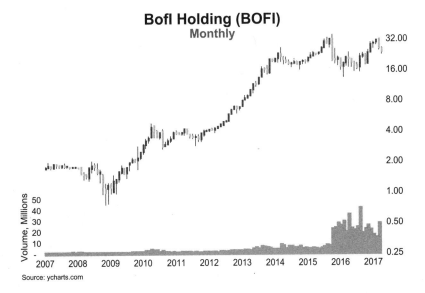

Source: ycharts.com

Figure 5-17

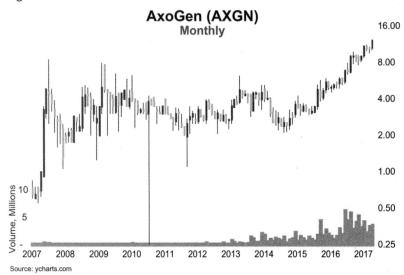

Figure 5-18

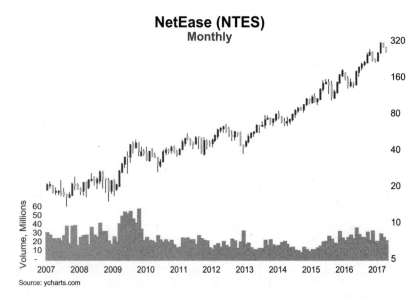

They say that the biggest opportunities are often outside of most people's comfort zones. The juiciest market returns are where very few are willing to go. Momentum investing is the ultimate contrarian approach.

How many investors would venture to buy a stock that's already up 50% in the past six months? Psychologically, it's a lot harder to buy in this situation than to sell.

How ridiculous does it sound that stocks that went up 50% in the past six months are likely to outperform in the next six months? Stock-picking can't be that easy, right?

There has to be some complicated formula that takes into account hundreds of different criteria in order to have a chance at outperforming the market.

Sometimes the most effective methods are the simplest. Most people stay away from them exactly because they seem too simple to work. There's nothing magical about using past performance to select future winners. It's all about simple math.

What do stocks that go up 200% in a year have in common?

Let's forget about size for a moment. Small-cap, small-float stocks are more volatile and more likely to experience larger moves, to the upside and the downside.

What else do the best-performing stocks of each year have in common? It's not that they started their moves from new 52-week highs. In fact, some of them started from 52-week lows, typically after the end of a major correction.

Before every stock reaches a 200% return for a given year, it's up only 50% at some point in that year.

Not all stocks that are up 50% in the past six months will continue higher. In fact, some of them will prove to be terrible losers.

But how do we know in advance which stocks that are already up 50% will continue higher and which stocks will inevitably reverse and go lower?

There are ways to substantially improve the odds of catching stocks with high potential to go a lot higher (which we cover later in this chapter). But the truth to the matter is that anything could happen. We don't know the future. And we don't have to.

Using proper risk-management tools is often just as good (and useful) as knowing the future.

We dive deeper into the ocean of risk management in Chapters Seven and Eight, but here's a brief overview.

The purpose of risk management is, well, to manage risk:

- To make sure we pick stocks that have the potential to appreciate substantially.

- To make sure our inevitable mistakes don't hurt our returns too much.

- To make sure we stay with our winning stocks long enough to make a difference in our returns.

- To make sure our winners are significantly bigger than our losers.

- To make sure our position sizing doesn't hurt our performance, our sleep, and our confidence.

- To be active in the market when it's worth being active, and to do nothing when there's nothing to do.

Here's a hypothetical example of how proper risk management could help you.

Let's assume you have $200,000 and you allocate $20,000 to 10 stocks that meet your criteria. Three of them keep going up and deliver 50% returns, while you're wrong on the other seven but limit your losses to 6% on each of them. What would be the end result?

Here's the math:

- A 50% return on a $20,000 allocation is $10,000

- A 6% loss on a $20,000 allocation is -$1,200

- $(3 \times 10{,}000) - (7 \times 1{,}200) = 30{,}000 - 8{,}400 = \$21{,}600$

The beauty of the stock market is that you don't have to be right very often in order to make a lot of money consistently.

There are people who are right only 30% of the time and still make millions every year. It's not important whether you're right or whether you're wrong. What matters is how much money you make when you're right and how much money you lose when you're wrong.

Sometimes you'll make a lot of money by blindly following a breakout in a momentum stock. Sometimes you'll lose. How much you lose and how much you make will depend on two factors: the market and you.

It isn't true that you decide how much you lose and the market decides how much you make. Nope. A stock could triple, but it's up to you when you sell. You could sell when it's up only 20%, having no clue what the future holds.

In our hypothetical case, you were right on only 30% of your picks, but you still managed to achieve a decent return on your capital. What's the flaw of this example?

While we could keep our losers small on most occasions, we have much less control over the size of our winners. They could be 50% or 5%.

Well, this is why we pick from the bucket with stocks that are already up 50% in the past six months.

Stocks that are up 50% in the past six months usually have something big going for them. It could be people's stupidity, but more often than not there's a good, fundamental reason: acceleration in earnings growth, a better-than-expected earnings report, industry momentum. We might not know the exact reason, but we know that someone has been accumulating them.

Stocks that are already up 50% in the past six months have the potential to be either huge winners or big losers in the next six months. When we add a layer of risk management, we make sure that our losers are manageable and that our winners will be worth it. You could rightfully claim that the same logic applies to any market method.

It's true: Proper risk management is that powerful.

We're not simply buying any stock that's up 50% in the past six months. We just keep an eye on them and engage only when there's a breakout to a new 52-week high (sometimes a new 50-day high) from a proper technical base.

The 52-week High List: Your Biggest Friend, Your Biggest Foe

Sometimes the 52-week high list is a shortcut to the minds of some of the smartest people in the world — people who see trends before everyone else and discount them in advance.

The rest of the time the 52-week list is often a reflection of people's greed, unreasonable expectations, and outright stupidity.

When a stock reaches a new 52-week high, it means that someone has just paid a price that no one has ever paid for an entire year. Does that make him or her smart or irresponsible? It depends on the context.

Amazon was considered insanely expensive when it hit a new all-time high of $110 in 2009. It remained "expensive" all the way up to $900 in 2017.

Many believed Apple was a can't-lose stock when it hit a new all-time high of $700 in September 2012 ($100 on a split-adjusted basis). It remained a "bargain" all the way down to $400 in the summer of 2013 ($57 adjusted for a 7-for-1 split). After 40% drawdown, it managed to recover to new all-time highs.

Which new 52-week or all-time high is the beginning and which is the end of a journey?

Warren Buffett likes to joke that a bull market is like sex: It feels best just before the end. Many gigantic trends have started with a new all-time high, but many trends have finished when there wasn't a single cloud in the sky.

Don't forget the stock market is one big house of mirrors, where many follow few. Almost no one is doing any real homework. Everyone is throwing a thesis on the wall hoping it'll stick. Everyone is faking it until someone makes it. No one knows the future. No one is right all the time.

Not all 52-week highs will turn into big winners. Sometimes you'll buy a breakout to new highs that will have all the characteristics of past winners, and you'll still lose money. It's part of the game. Accept it and move on. The next big mover is right around the corner.

All big stock market winners appear multiple times on the new 52-week high list, but not all stocks that appear on the new high list turn into big winners. When you "shop" from the 52-week high list, you're shopping from a list of potential winners.

The question is, which ones are going to continue to outperform? Which new all-time high is going to turn into the next 200% or 1,000% gainer? While we can't know that with any degree of certainty, there are ways to improve the odds in our favor.

The Magic Number

Three main factors will help you improve your odds of finding big winners.

Perspective

The 52-week high list is a raw data point, which could be enormously useful if you know how to read it properly. Context is much more important than the data.

If a stock is up 800% in the past three years, perhaps the market has gone too much ahead of itself. If it's over-followed by analysts and over-owned by institutions, the risk of owning might be greater than the potential returns.

Of course we never know how far a trend could go and how long it could last, but a proper entry point could improve our odds.

Catalysts

Price often moves before any change in fundamentals, and yet some catalysts improve the odds of finding a winner with significant upside potential.

Some catalysts have the rare impact of turning sidelined spectators into buyers and forcing short-sellers to cover their bets:

- When a breakout from a proper base is accompanied by a report of accelerating earnings growth that's better than expected, the odds are that we have a stock that's likely to sustain its move and go higher over time.

- When a breakout is in a currently hot industry, the odds are that it will follow through and deliver gains far exceeding the risk taken.

Technical Patterns

We don't know where in its trend we're buying a stock, but this doesn't mean we have to chase. We always look for a base that could define our risk.

Why is buying a breakout from a proper technical base important? Because the formation of a base means that there's someone accumulating the stock. Investors (institutions) wouldn't accumulate a stock if they didn't expect its price to go higher.

Their expectations could be founded on pure speculation or on sophisticated and comprehensive market research. There's no guarantee that they'll end up being right and that we're going to make money following their footsteps, reflected in stock charts.

We don't need to be right every time in order to consistently make money. The existence of a proper technical base helps us to define where we are wrong and where we should exit.

The same patterns repeat over and over again. The only things that change are the names of the stocks behind them.

We look for two major types of patterns:

- **Continuation:** Stocks with established uptrends that are breaking out to new 52-week highs (or at least new 50-day highs) from tight bases on a weekly time frame.

- **The beginning of a new trend:** Stocks that break out to new 52-week highs from a multi-month-long base on at least three times their average daily volume.

Here are 12 annotated charts illustrating both patterns, including where to enter and where to set your initial stop.

Figure 5-19

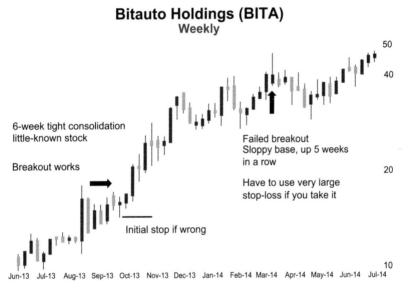

Bitauto Holdings (BITA)
Weekly

6-week tight consolidation
little-known stock

Breakout works

Failed breakout
Sloppy base, up 5 weeks
in a row

Have to use very large
stop-loss if you take it

Initial stop if wrong

Jun-13 Jul-13 Aug-13 Sep-13 Oct-13 Nov-13 Dec-13 Jan-14 Feb-14 Mar-14 Apr-14 May-14 Jun-14 Jul-14

Source: ycharts.com

Figure 5-20

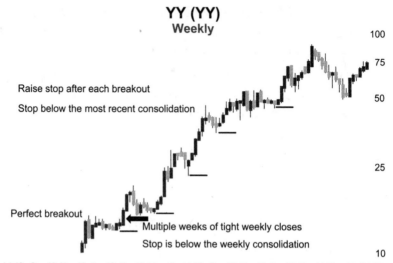

Source: ycharts.com

Figure 5-21

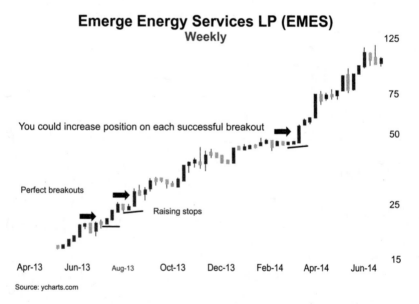

Source: ycharts.com

Figure 5-22

Canadian Solar, Inc. (CSIQ)
Weekly

Sloppy wide-range bases, but breakouts work because of strong industry momentum.

Apr-12 Jun-12 Aug-12 Oct-12 Dec-12 Feb-13 Apr-13 Jun-13 Aug-13 Oct-13 Dec-13 Feb-14

Source: ycharts.com

Figure 5-23

Grupo Financiero Galicia (GGAL)
Weekly

Breakout from a perfect base

Stop

Jun-13 Aug-13 Oct-13 Dec-13 Feb-14 Apr-14 Jun-14 Aug-14 Oct-14 Dec-14 Feb-15

Source: ycharts.com

Figure 5-24

Figure 5-25

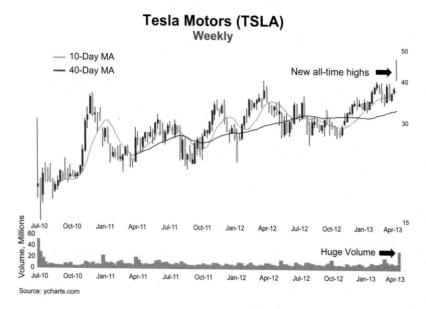

Figure 5-26

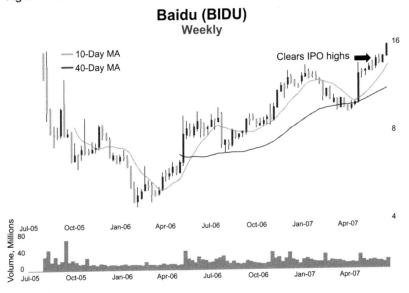

Baidu (BIDU)
Weekly

Source: ycharts.com

Figure 5-27

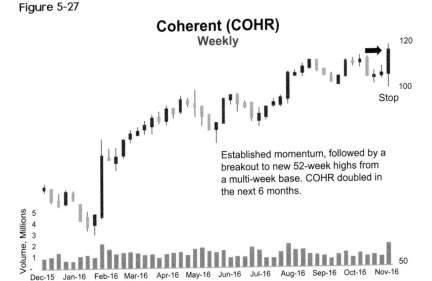

Coherent (COHR)
Weekly

Established momentum, followed by a
breakout to new 52-week highs from
a multi-week base. COHR doubled in
the next 6 months.

Source: ycharts.com

Figure 5-28

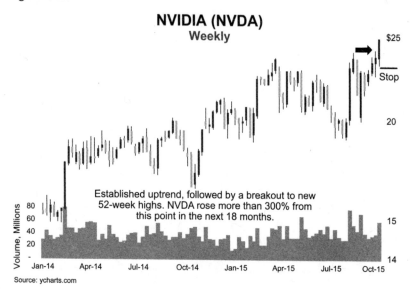

Established uptrend, followed by a breakout to new
52-week highs. NVDA rose more than 300% from
this point in the next 18 months.

Source: ycharts.com

Figure 5-29

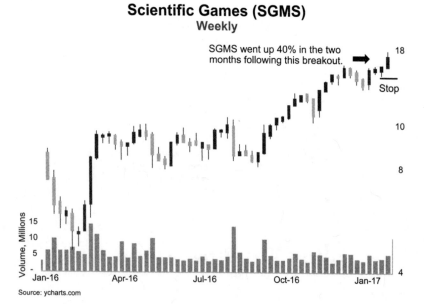

Source: ycharts.com

Figure 5-30

What about the 52-week Low List?

Stay away from stocks making new 52-week lows in a bull market. They're usually there for a good reason.

Yes, you'll miss the beginning of some turnaround stories. But you'll save yourself a lot of trouble and, in general, you'll do your portfolio a huge favor.

If a rising tide can't lift a particular boat, that boat probably has serious leaks. It's the same in the stock market: If a raging bull market can't push a stock from its 52-week low, there's probably something inherently wrong with the business of the underlying company.

It's always tempting to buy a stock that has declined 50% from its 52-week high level, but it's rarely a good idea if the drop occurs in the midst of a bull market.

Many tried to catch the bottom in coal stocks after they plunged 50% in 2011. Then they dropped another 50% in 2012 and another 50% by mid-2014 and yet another 70% by early 2015.

When all was said and done (and we don't know if it's over yet), the majority of coal stocks were trading 95% below their all-time highs from 2011. In the midst of one of the biggest bull markets in financial history, coal stocks simply obliterated the capital of everyone who tried to catch their bottom.

Don't be greedy about turnaround situations in bull markets. They say that we should buy low expectations, and the 52-week low list is the ultimate symbol of low market expectations. The thing is that a stock that looks cheap could get a lot cheaper before it recovers.

Big price declines are usually followed by a long period of sideways action, during which most market participants lose interest. Believe it or not, some stocks go to zero, and those that usually do spend a lot of time on the 52-week low list before they file for bankruptcy.

Even if they don't go to zero, it might take years to recover. During that time, you could allocate your capital to a lot more productive assets, save yourself countless headaches, and actually make money.

As the saying about stocks in a downtrend goes, if they don't scare you out, they'll wear you out.

Buying 52-week lows during bear markets is a completely different matter. When the general market goes down 20%, even the stocks of the strongest companies could decline substantially. There are some incredible bargains on the 52-week low list during periods of forced liquidation.

But how do you recognize the ones that are likely to bounce and recover to new highs and the ones that are struggling for a good reason? You don't have to. You could simply wait for them to hit new 52-week highs.

In fact, the ones that hit this benchmark first as the general market tries to recover are likely to be the leaders of the next bull market — the stocks that you must own if you want to achieve outsized returns. We elaborate on this subject in Chapter Seven.

Resources

There are numerous free or really cheap sources for the 52-week high list, including finviz.com, chartmill.com, barchart.com, investors. com, wsj.com, nasdaq.com, etc.

There will be times when the 52-week high list has hundreds and even thousands of names every day, and it will be hard to sift through all the opportunities. This is a good problem to have. It's a sign of an expanding risk appetite, but it's a real challenge nevertheless.

If you would like to take a shortcut, consider signing up for the Social Leverage 50 (marketwisdom.com), which features 50 stocks trading near multi-year highs and possessing great prospects to substantially outperform the market averages.

SIX

How to Find the Best-Performing Stocks in Any Given Year

"To make money, you must find something that nobody else knows, or do something that others won't do because they have rigid mind-sets."

— Peter Lynch

"Participants act not on the basis of their best interests but on their perception of their best interests, and the two are not identical."

— George Soros

How It Works

There's a saying that, in the stock market, the obvious rarely happens and the unexpected constantly occurs. Nothing else describes better the true nature of the market. It could sometimes be quite counterintuitive.

The biggest opportunities are often disguised and exist in industries most people aren't willing to touch.

In 2012, the conventional wisdom was to stay away from all Chinese stocks. China's economy was slowing down. Its stock market was a mess. Earnings numbers were questionable.

As a result, only two China-based American Depositary Receipts (ADRs) made their debuts on U.S. exchanges that year, Vipshop Holdings and YY Inc. Both of them formed solid technical bases, broke out to new all-time highs, and never looked back.

Don't assume you know everything. The market is frequently a lot wiser than you and discounts events and processes long before they become mainstream. What you don't know won't hurt you, but what you think you know when it isn't so will. Don't let your biases blind you. Pay attention to price action.

It happens over and over again, and it will continue to happen, because that's how financial markets work.

Figure 6-1

Vipshop Holdings (VIPS)
Weekly

Source: ycharts.com

Figure 6-2

YY (YY)
Monthly

Source: ycharts.com

We constantly watch the all-time high and the 52-week high lists to get a sense of emerging trends and to gauge overall risk appetite. Both lists are extremely useful equity selection tools, and they've been home to all big stock market winners at some point in their history.

An all-time high is not an automatic buy signal for us. We've always considered the technical characteristics of the stock. We also pay attention to the catalyst behind the breakout and the growth prospects of the underlying company and its industry.

All those requirements have proven to be good filters over time — but at the cost of numerous unwanted side effects.

Here's how overthinking has robbed us of some great market opportunities.

In February 2011 tobacco stocks were clearing major multi-year highs on strong volume.

Figure 6-3

We disregarded the signal, conceptualizing that smoking is dying and that tobacco companies will only see their revenues decline. Philip Morris, Lorillard, and Altria gained more than 50% in the next year.

Figure 6-4

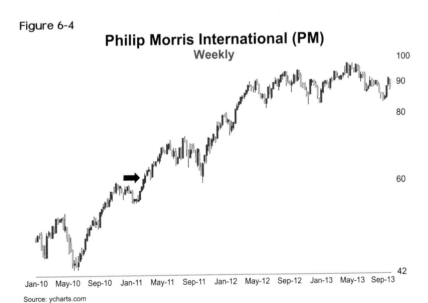

In June 2011 we noticed that more and more utilities were showing up on the all-time high list. We knew that it was never a good sign
when defensive stocks were on the all-time high list, but we'd never really considered owning them, because they weren't real growth stocks.

Many of those same utilities went on to significantly outperform
during the carnage of summer 2011, as capital fled to perceived safety.

In September 2011 a bunch of real estate investment trusts (REITs)
and home improvement stores (Home Depot, Lowes) were breaking
out to major multi-year highs. We ignored those moves, thinking that
no one wanted to own those slow-moving, boring stocks.

Figure 6-5

Besides, we reasoned, there was no way those moves could be
sustained, with housing prices still under pressure at the time. Many
of them went up 30%-plus over the next six months, as Home Depot
reported solid earnings growth and rents reached all-time highs all
over the U.S. Even homebuilders like Lennar started to emerge to new
highs in early 2012.

Figure 6-6

Home Depot (HD)
Weekly

Source: ycharts.com

In April 2012 airline stocks were showing up on the 52-week high list. Inconceivable!

Figure 6-7

Alaska Air Group (ALK)
Weekly

Source: ycharts.com

We quickly disregarded those moves as noise, recalling that airlines had historically been terrible investments. Two years later, all airline stocks had more than doubled.

Figure 6-8

Alaska Air Group (ALK)
Weekly

Jan-12 Apr-12 Jul-12 Oct-12 Jan-13 Apr-13 Jul-13 Oct-13 Jan-14 Apr-14 Jul-14 Oct-14 Jan-15
Source: ycharts.com

In hindsight everything seems so clear. But in real time it's never so easy. The point is that we have no idea how far a stock might go after it breaks out to all-time highs from a solid base. It might go up 15% and then fizzle, or it might go up 50% or 200%. We don't know that in advance, and we have no control over it.

Good risk/reward technical signals have to be taken. Focusing on price action alone helps to minimize any underlying biases.

When you find yourself surprised to see certain stocks on the 52-week high list, there are two possibilities:

- You don't know the whole story. Your perception is worse than the reality. The market might be discounting something you don't know or fully understand yet.

- Whatever it is you think you know doesn't currently matter. The worst has already been discounted. Everyone who wanted to sell has already sold, and a whole new set of buyers is now stepping in, changing entirely the supply/demand dynamics.

What Do You Know, What Don't You Know

What hurts you is not what you don't know. What hurts you is what you think you know that is not true.

If you let this concept become a cornerstone of your market philosophy, it will become a lot easier to find and own stocks that are likely to deliver substantial returns.

Why is this so?

Because in any given year, the best-performing stocks are the ones that surprise the most, the ones for which expectations are very low and yet start to rise in price.

Expectations could be low for two basic reasons:

- A stock is neglected. No one is paying attention to it. It's often trading under $10. It has a small float and market cap, and its daily volume is relatively low. Liquidity often follows price momentum, and price momentum follows change. Sudden change means opportunity.

- The stock of interest and its industry are universally hated.

Some of the biggest mistakes in our investing lives are often mistakes by omission. The biggest regrets always come from positions we could have taken but for subjective reasons and irrational biases we did not.

Don't assume you know everything. The market is frequently a lot wiser than you and discounts events and processes long before they become mainstream. Don't let your biases blind you. Pay attention to price action.

The more you think you know, the more closed-minded you are, and that poses a two-fold danger.

Overconfidence in your current positions will blind you to potential threats.

Overconfidence in your current positions will also blind you to great market opportunities.

If your approach tells you to buy a stock and you ignore it because of personal biases, you should force yourself to buy it anyway. The odds are that a lot of other investors will feel the same way and are going to pass on that opportunity.

As Jesse Livermore put it, "Successful trading is always an emotional battle, not a battle of intelligence."

If you want to make a lot of money in the stock market, you have to do something that most are not willing to do.

The best-performing stocks in any given year are the ones that surprise the most, which means that they are very likely to come from an industry almost no one expects.

In late 2011 housing-related stocks started to clear 52-week highs. No one believed in their moves because of their horrid performance in the previous few years. They ended up being the hottest sector in 2012.

Solar stocks were left for dead between 2009 and 2012. Things took a 180-degree spin in early 2013, when many of them broke out to new 52-week highs.

No one trusted these range expansions. In most people's minds solar stocks were still untouchable garbage. By the end of the year many of them more than tripled.

The surprise factor is the essence behind this approach. There are two ways a stock could shock the street:

- When it reports a much better than expected earnings and sales number, which sparks a rally in its entire industry. The initial market reaction is what's important here. If the market doesn't care, we don't care, and we move on.

- It comes from an industry no one expects to be performing well. The market is often a forward-looking mechanism that discounts six to 12 months in advance.

As Howard Marks likes to repeat, "The big winners come from the so-called high-risk categories, but the risks have more to do with the investors' perception than with the categories."

One of the most powerful combinations of catalysts is a new 52-week high plus high short interest plus very negative sentiment, so negative people don't even want to listen to you when you start talking about that industry.

The only way to make big money in the market is by being right about something that the majority of people have gotten wrong.

The patterns repeat over and over again. The only things that change are the names involved. Everyone hated banks in 2010-11. No one wanted to touch them because they were all considered black boxes, and the market always pays lower valuation for higher uncertainty.

Meanwhile, a small, San Diego-based bank was breaking out to new annual highs. When the whole sector started to lift on the good news flow from the housing sector, Bank of the Internet (BofI Holdings) just went ballistic, from $17 to $46 in a year.

Figure 6-9

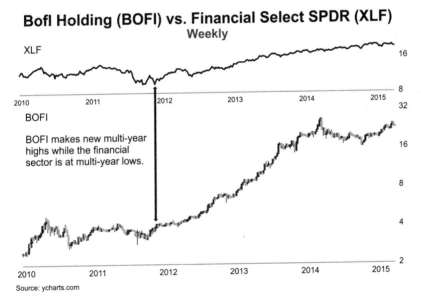

BofI Holding (BOFI) vs. Financial Select SPDR (XLF)
Weekly

BOFI makes new multi-year highs while the financial sector is at multi-year lows.

Source: ycharts.com

Over time, we noticed that if we hated the stocks that have technically perfect breakouts, the odds are that we've found some great winners. Think about it: The only reason to hate an industry is because of
a bias that has been built by the media.

From a sentimental point of view, we want to buy when an asset is
ridiculed. For practical purposes, we add a new high as a filter.

We want to own them at the right time, so our capital works for us
instead of getting stuck in trendless consolidations or, worse, in positions that go against us.

About That List

Here are three reasons why the 52-week high list is so important.

- We don't want to be first. We want to be in stocks that move, and
being on the 52-week high list attracts a lot of attention.
- It's an important benchmark, followed by many investors.
- You can't make a cent before the market agrees with you. The
market's way of agreeing with you is by sending your stock to
the 52-week high list.

The market is often forward-looking, and it discounts events that
have not happened yet. This is why sometimes you'll see stocks breaking out on the 52-week high list but you'll have no clue what they're
doing there.

This is a good thing. By the time the reason behind a move is clear
to everyone, most of this move will likely be over. This is just how the
market works. You could accept it and adjust, or you could look for
another field to apply your intellect. Warren Buffett likes to joke that if
you have an IQ of 160, you could give away 30 points and you'd still
be a very successful investor.

The only reason two people perceive the same situation differently
is because they have different experiences. When you have different
experiences, you have different expectations and act differently.

When a stock or an industry that's widely hated or massively
neglected starts making new 52-week highs, someone must be seeing

something the majority isn't. It takes real buying power for such a stock to break out to new 52-week highs.

Something must've changed for a stock to hit a new 52-week high. Somebody is buying. We already talked about the notion that the 52-week high list could sometimes be considered a shortcut to the minds of smart people, a place where we can read their investment theses and understand the trends that they are seeing and trying to discount.

If so many people hate the stock and the industry, why are they not impacting its price negatively? The reasons are very simple.

Those who are short are already short. They've already sold with an intention to buy back at lower prices. They have no impact on supply anymore.

In fact, past short-selling is a source of future demand. The stock is already at new 52-week highs, so most of the short-sellers are likely under water. The first new 52-week high doesn't discourage them.

On the contrary, some of them will probably double down and short more. They're the source that will fuel the rally in the future as the stock keeps going persistently higher.

Those who had been burned by the stock or the industry in the past couple years are totally indifferent to what's currently going on. They don't want to hear about it. They don't care. They don't believe.

When an asset is down big several years in a row, we could make the rational assumption that almost everyone who wanted to sell has already done so. Those still playing are day- and swing-traders, who are renters and don't own it for more than a few days.

Considering all those factors, it takes only a very little bump in demand for prices to rise. Such a bump could be caused by two factors:

- A surprising earnings report or new business contract that totally changes expectations and perceptions. Prices change when expectations change.

- Smart people start buying in anticipation of future positive catalysts.

We look for situations where the perception is worse than the reality.

We don't buy stocks that are out of fashion. We buy stocks that are hated, highly shorted, and ridiculed... and that are making new 52-week highs.

We don't buy low expectations. We buy bearish sentiment and indifference plus rising expectations plus new 52-week highs.

There's a difference between perceptions and expectations: The former deals with the present, the latter with the future.

Our expectations are based on our experience in similar situations. Why would a highly hated stock make a new 52-week high? Apparently, people who've been through many recovery processes before and understand the cyclical nature of market psychology see potential in the stock and are willing to put their money to work. Otherwise prices wouldn't be rising.

In a situation where there's very little supply, it doesn't take much demand to lift prices higher. Everyone who wanted to sell and take the loss has already done so. And almost everyone who wanted to go short has done so too. The short interest is, therefore, over 15%, and the cost of borrowing is extremely high.

A stock could make a new 52-week high on the basis of the rising expectations of select forward-looking individuals, while the general public doesn't pay attention and is indifferent.

A new 52-week high from a proper technical base garnished with negative sentiment is one of the most powerful combinations.

New 52-week highs plus outsized skepticism and outright ridicule is a very powerful equity selection combination.

The best-performing stocks in any given year will have those same characteristics. They'll keep going higher, and people will keep making fun of them and even try to short them and say that this is only a short-term blip and the stock is bound to reverse lower.

The media won't even pay attention to it. Indifference and low press coverage is good.

Every truth goes through three stages. At first it's ridiculed, then it's violently opposed, and, eventually, it's accepted as self-evident. The best-performing stocks in any single year go through those three stages. We want to own them when they are ridiculed and start to gradually scale out when their trend is accepted as given and self-evident.

The trend doesn't end in the third stage. It accelerates and gets a lot more violent and noticeable. The press coverage increases substantially, not only from specialized financial papers like *Investor's Business Daily*, *The Wall Street Journal*, *Bloomberg News*, and *The Financial Times* but also in more mainstream press sources.

A trend could continue a lot longer than most people expect. We don't sell an entire position when everyone starts to like it. We start to slowly scale out. We sell 20% here and there for the sake of locking in some profit.

With this approach you only need to find one or two industries per year to achieve substantial returns. Focus on where the money is going, and, if that place is universally hated and ridiculed, buy as much as your risk-management approach allows and make sure you make some real money.

It's a philosophy that should serve you well for the rest of your investing life. The more you practice it, the better you'll become at executing it.

Turnaround Situations Need Catalysts

Price is the ultimate catalyst.

Sometimes a widely neglected industry will start making new 52-week highs before the underlying companies report any notable change in growth. In such cases a few forward-looking people with purchasing power are positioning for a major change, as happened with housing stocks in 2012, including Home Depot and Lennar, and select banks in 2011, like BofI Holdings..

Other times an unexpected strong earnings report will cause a sudden gap to major new highs and this will be the beginning of a major turnaround situation, as was the case with Netflix, First Solar, SunPower, and Keurig Green Mountain.

Almost all stocks eventually make new 52-week highs in a bull market, including some really crappy businesses, and that new 52-week high would look like a turnaround situation. How do you distinguish between the real turn-around situations, which could deliver 500% return in a year, and the high-flyers that are likely to give back quickly what they have gained?

There are two important arguments to cover here.

Here's the first. We could filter by focusing on stocks of companies that have just reported better-than-expected earnings. We could focus only on stocks that are lifted with their entire industries.

The second begins with a question: What's the difference between a stock going up 300% and then giving back most of it and a stock that appreciated 300% and then stays there for a while? For you as a market participant, it shouldn't matter much. You could make a lot of money in both cases. Every trend eventually comes to an end, but this doesn't mean that you should give all your gains back.

When a stock that's been a disappointment for a few years suddenly appears on the 52-week high list, it'll attract a lot of attention. If a stock that only a few months ago was the butt of jokes in the investor community suddenly starts making new highs it's huge news.

Most people will be extremely skeptical, but this is exactly what you want to see in a trend. Every trend needs skeptics and disbelievers; otherwise, there won't be anyone left to buy.

Why do people hate this kind of a stock? The answer is very simple: It has underperformed and disappointed for a long period of time. The media has written a ton of negative articles about it. In a way, the perception has become worse than the reality. The worst-case scenario has been discounted.

Remember that the market tends to over-discount identified risks. This is one explanation why stocks that are dropped from the Nasdaq 100 during the end of the year rebalancing tend to outperform the next year.

The stocks that are dropped are always among the worst performers of the current year. Many funds sell them for tax-loss purposes to a
point that they become a bargain for value-hunting investors.

The removal from the Nasdaq 100 is the crescendo of a bad year
— an event that could only be described as sell the rumors, buy the
news.

Sentiment Cycle in a Typical Turnaround Situation

All stocks are price-cyclical. Upside and downside momentum
beyond three years often leads to mean-reversion, especially when it
comes to whole sectors and industries.

The way most people react to price action is very similar, and that
reaction hasn't altered during the entire history of equity markets. It
hasn't changed because human psychology has remained static. This
is why the same patterns repeat over and over again.

Figure 6-10

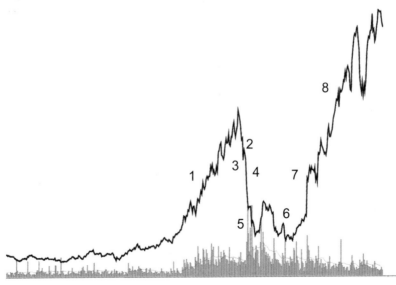

Here are the key points to know about the sentiment cycle:

1. A nice, steady uptrend forms. Everyone loves the industry.

2. The trend is over.

3. Knife-catchers are getting slaughtered.

4. There are very few buyers. Momentum guys are out or short. Value guys aren't interested. Everyone rushes through the exit.

5. People are making fun of the industry. It's "dead," for good.

6. Indifference. No one cares about it. If it's mentioned, it's to make fun of it. Everyone agrees it has no future. The stage of indifference could last anywhere between a few months to a few quarters. It'll also be reflected in the smaller trading volume and number of analysts that follow the group.

7. A new point of interest forms. It suddenly makes a new multi-month high on relatively big volume.

8. Many won't believe this move and will fight it on the way up, creating conditions for a further short squeeze. Many will be afraid to enter because "it's up too much, too fast."

There's a small but very important detail here. You don't go and buy all stocks that are down 90% in the past three years. You wait for a new 52-week high or at least new 50-day highs from a proper base on huge volume before you go long.

Having a fundamental catalyst like a big earnings surprise behind a breakout to new 52-week highs improves substantially the odds of finding a big winner.

A dog can remain a dog a lot longer than most people expect. Remember the new 52-week high requirement. Without it, nothing else matters. We want price momentum on our side. We want price to confirm our thesis.

Some people like to say that they look to buy low expectations, not low prices, but keep in mind that low expectations aren't a catalyst. They're just a measure of the potential move once a real catalyst is presented.

P/E ratios and price action don't necessarily measure expectations. Expectations are measured by sentiment. Different people have different expectations due to different backgrounds and market philosophies.

What we want is an asset that separates the opinion. Consensus opinions are dangerous and often already discounted. We want stocks that are rising in price and on which analysts totally disagree.

At the early stages of Tesla's appreciation, analysts had no idea how to value it. The range in analysts' projections was $15 billion in market cap terms, which was as much as what the company was worth at the time. These are characteristics of a stock that deserves our special attention.

We look for an upside move (defined by a new 52-week high) in a previously neglected stock that's so surprising no one believes it. Such a setup means two things:

- Early longs are eager to sell and pocket profits. If this initial buying pressure couldn't hold the stock of interest and it continues to go higher, it's a clear indication that someone with a lot of purchasing power is accumulating.
- New short-sellers start to appear.

In early 2013 we wrote that solar stocks would be to 2013 what housing-related stocks were to 2012: the best performers coming from a place no one expects.

We didn't believe enough in our arguments, so we were early sellers, and we traded in and out of the solar names rather than holding them for a longer period of time. In strong, trending markets, sitting with your big winners is what makes you the most money.

In low-volatility, trending markets, you'll regret selling too early. In high-volatility, mean-reversion markets, you'll regret selling too late.

The lesson: The best-performing stocks in any given year often come from industries that no one expects.

Be open-minded. When you see widely disliked stocks breaking out to new 52-week highs from perfect technical bases, buy some.

When you buy and people make fun of you, make sure to buy some more. When someone you consider very smart tells you that you're crazy for buying them, go and buy some more.

Having people disagree with your investment thesis while your stocks are making new 52-week highs is the most beautiful thing that could happen to you.

Every trend needs skeptics and doubters. Otherwise there wouldn't be anyone left to buy.

You Can't Achieve Big Returns by Following the Conventional Wisdom

They say that two types of people are the most dangerous in the stock market: those who know nothing and those who act like they know everything.

The more important question is this: Who are the types of people that make the most money in the stock market?

We say they're those who have a very good understanding of how markets work and those who end up being right about something about which the majority of people are wrong.

If you want to achieve outsized returns, you have to do something that most people aren't willing to do. If something feels psychologically difficult to do in the stock market, it's often the right thing to do. If it were easy, everyone would do it, and the end result would therefore be nothing spectacular.

Doing something psychologically difficult doesn't guarantee you success, but it does guarantee you outsized returns if you end up being right. The only way to make big money is to be right about something about which almost everyone else is wrong.

If you're right about something about which everyone else is right too, you'll only achieve average returns. Sometimes being average isn't a bad outcome, but we're striving for more than that.

What are some of the signs that other people aren't on the same page as you?

They'll tell you. Your idea will seem so ridiculous to them that they'll make fun of it. You know what? This is a really good sign. It means that you're onto something big. It means that, if you're right, your payback will be huge.

Being a contrarian doesn't always work, but when it does the payoff is ginormous.

You can't make big money conventionally. If everyone believes an asset is a great buy, their beliefs are very likely to already be reflected in the price of this asset. Everyone already owns it.

If, on the other hand, almost everyone believes an asset is a terrible buy and yet it makes a new 52-week high, it's probably well worth our consideration.

If you catch yourself not wanting to take a new 52-week high because of what you've heard in the media, the odds are that you've encountered a big future winner. Many other investors have probably been brainwashed the same way you were, and this is why everyone is skeptical when the stock of interest makes new highs.

The existence of pessimists is a necessary condition for the durability of trends.

We always smile when we see people making fun of or questioning our investment ideas. It tells us that we're probably on the right path.

We have a very clear rule of thumb: Any time we see a perfect technical setup and we catch ourselves not wanting to buy the stock, because of personal, irrational biases (we don't like the company, the management, the industry, etc.), we force ourselves to take the position. We know that the odds are good that we're onto something great.

This is how investing works. It has to be a little counterintuitive.

As Howard Marks notes in *The Most Important Thing*:

When everyone believes something is risky, their unwillingness to buy usually reduces its price to the point where it's not risky at all. Broadly negative opinion can make it the least risky thing, since all optimism has been driven out of its price.

Marks looks at contrarianism from a value point of view. We like to view contrarianism from a momentum point of view.

We assume it's really hard for many people to buy an asset when it's down 90% from its highs and has kept going down for many months, even years. Or, maybe, it's easier, because it seems cheaper.

What we know is that it's always an emotional struggle to buy a stock when it's up 100% in the past six months and it's at all-time highs. And yet this is exactly how many multi-year leaders begin the journey of their super-performance.

No one has ever made a killing by going with the consensus, but there are many people who have lost their fortunes by going against the crowd. Our goal is not to be contrarian for the sake of being contrarian. We do it with only one intention: to make money.

There's a huge difference between thinking contrarian and acting contrarian. The latter is a lot harder to implement because it goes against human nature.

More often than not being a contrarian means staying with the price trend. It means buying a stock when it makes new 52-week highs and it comes from an industry most are afraid to touch.

SEVEN

There Is Always a Silver Lining

"It is not entirely clear what causes deep market corrections, but without them many of the best performing long-term investors would have never achieved their spectacular returns."

— Peter Lynch

"Headlines, in a way, are what mislead you, because bad news is a headline, and gradual improvement is not."

— Bill Gates

A Glass Half Full, But With What?

Why is it always 30% chance of rain and never 70% chance of sun?

Blame it on the weathermen, but this is a good example of how our society decodes new information. We're biologically wired to pay more attention to scary headlines, and, as a result the media bombards us with pessimism.

Somehow the mainstream press always finds a way to put a negative spin on every piece of economic data. If retail sales are down, the consumer isn't buying and the economy might be entering recession. If retail sales are up, there's a threat of inflation. If oil prices rise too fast, it's bad for the economy because it will diminish the purchasing power of the consumer. If oil prices fall too quickly, it's a sign of a slowing economy.

What's wrong with these people?

In 2014 the Russia-based news website *The City Reporter* decided to perform a social experiment. It reported only good news for an entire day. It only featured positive stories and gave silver linings to all negative stories.

For example, it ran a story headlined "No disruption on roads despite snow."

The results were catastrophic for the website's traffic. *The City Reporter* lost two-thirds of its normal readership that day.

At the end of the day the majority of journalists and media people are interested in catching people's attention. An article with a warning and negative spin on any news does a great job achieving that, but it's rarely a good source of investment advice.

Ignore grandiose, negative headlines. Wildly optimistic headlines could be just as dangerous, but this is a topic for another discussion.

There's a better way to look at the world and think deeply about your investments. We call it "the glass half full" approach.

By no means is it an approach based on wishful thinking and day-dreaming. It comes from a simple understanding of how markets function. Every company's rising cost is another company's rising revenue. And the opposite is also true: Every company's declining revenue is another company's declining cost.

And do you know what the best part is? The stock market usually does a good job of recognizing the beneficiaries in every situation by sending their stocks to the 52-week high list.

Take advantage of it.

Money Never Sleeps

Every crisis brings an opportunity. Every bust in one area of financial markets puts the foundations for a boom in another area. Money never sleeps. It constantly goes somewhere — sometimes for rational reasons, other times because of sheer speculation.

Nevertheless, as long as humans are involved in financial markets, there will be booms and busts, crises and recoveries.

America went into recession in the early 2000s, and Americans went to school to gain another diploma. As a result, education stocks rallied to the sky. Between 2000 and 2004, shares of Apollo Education Group went from $10 to $100.

Terrorists hit the Twin Towers in 2001, and America went to war. As a result, defense stocks appreciated substantially. Between 2002 and 2005, shares of Kevlar® maker Ceradyne went up 1,800%.

The bust in tech stocks in the early 2000s alienated regular Americans from stocks, and they decided to put their money into houses. Homebuilders' stocks went up five times and more in a fairly short period of time, before they went bust.

Between 2001 and 2005 shares of Beazer Homes went from $40 to $370, Toll Brothers went from $7 to $50, and Ryland Group went from $7 to $80.

The Federal Reserve's aggressive monetary easing coupled with emerging markets' hunger for basic materials caused a massive spike in demand and inflation. As a result, commodities went through the roof. While market averages deteriorated in the first half of 2008, many basic material stocks quadrupled.

Yes, in the second half of 2008 they gave up most of their profits and then some more. But they created incredible opportunities for people who were simply following price trends and had an exit strategy. Between 2007 and mid-2008, shares of potash maker Mosaic went from $15 to $150.

The financial crisis of 2008-09 brought all stocks to their knees. Many small-caps were priced for bankruptcy. Most of them survived and went up more than 1,000% in the ensuing four to five years. Mattress maker Select Comfort was trading near 25 cents per share in early 2009. By 2012, it is trading near $35.

Big corrections create the opportunity for big recoveries.

The European sovereign bond crisis of 2011 and the overall slow employment recovery in the United States encouraged the Fed to launch a series of unprecedented monetary policy injections with the code name "quantitative easing."

Waves of capital flooded public and private markets and caused material appreciation in most financial assets.

Crude oil collapsed more than 50% between mid-2014 and early 2016. The energy crash set the foundations for some incredible wealth-building opportunities in U.S.-based and emerging-market commodity names. Resolute Energy went from $3 to $50 between June 2016 and February 2017. Clayton Williams Energy went from $8 to $150 between April and December 2016.

Embrace Market Corrections

We live in times of perpetual booms and busts that come one after another. In fact they cause each other.

Every five years or so there's a deep market pullback that creates incredible opportunities for savvy investors. Corrections make investors a lot of money. Most of them just don't know it at the time.

And we don't refer only to value investors, who are happy to buy high-quality businesses and distressed assets on the cheap. We also refer to momentum and growth investors.

In the fall of 2008 it felt like the financial world as we know it was going to end. Stocks were plunging every day, hit by waves of forced liquidation. Institutions were selling not because they wanted to but because they had to, due to redemptions from clients and margin calls.

Individual investors were scrambling to exit their shares at any price. They just wanted to be in cash. Who's to blame them? Companies that were considered indestructible filed for bankruptcy or their stocks collapsed more than 50%.

People were scared and didn't trust anyone.

In the midst of the biggest financial crisis since the Great Depression, Warren Buffett wrote an op-ed for *The New York Times* headlined "Buy American. I Am."

When volatility and correlations were at record-high levels, when most investors were running scared and couldn't sell their stocks fast enough, Buffett was buying with both hands.

Buffett was early. Stocks continued to decline for five more months and went a lot lower before they finally bottomed in March 2009. At that time many stocks, especially small-caps, were priced for bankruptcy, which never materialized. Over the following eight years stocks staged a massive rally. Quite a few went up 1,000% or more.

The beauty of the stock market is that you never have to be first in order to make a lot of money. In March 2009 you didn't have to guess which stocks were going to survive in order to profit from their recovery.

You could have achieved substantial returns by entering in the middle of their trends, when their existence was no longer questionable and when they were breaking out to new 52-week highs from proper bases.

Do you remember the first stocks to hit new all-time highs after the bottom in March 2009? As the major market indexes were making new lows every day in February and early March, a select group of stocks, such as Netflix, Keurig Green Mountain, and AutoZone, were trading tightly near their all-time highs.

As soon as the indexes bounced, those three stocks made new all-time highs. They ended up becoming some of the best performers in the first two years of the market recovery.

Patterns repeat, like clockwork, in financial markets. The only things that change are the names of the stocks that form them. What happened with Netflix and Keurig Green Mountain and AutoZone in 2009 has happened in every single correction in market history.

Stocks that show relative strength during major market pullbacks become the leaders of the next rally.

And the first stocks that break out to new 52-week highs after a correction often outperform substantially during the recovery.

Here are annotated examples illustrating the value of understanding relative strength and breakouts to new 52-week highs.

Figure 7-1

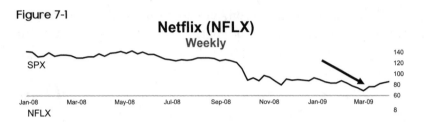

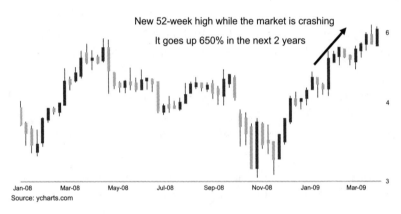

Source: ycharts.com

Figure 7-2

Source: ycharts.com

Figure 7-3

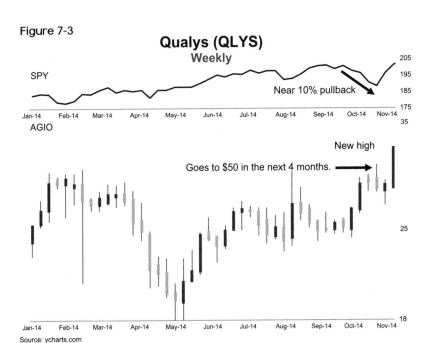

Source: ycharts.com

Figure 7-4

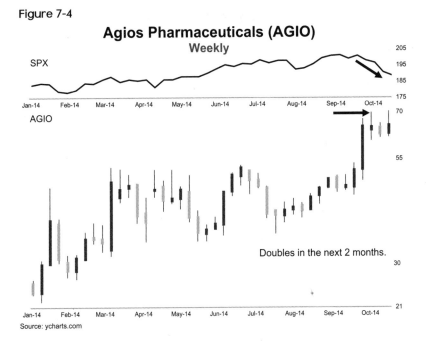

Source: ycharts.com

Figure 7-5

LendingTree (TREE)
Monthly

Big market correction give the opportunity to create
angel investment-like returns with a lot less risk, less
work and much higher success rate.

TREE went up more than 100x
between early 2009 and 2015.

Source: ycharts.com

Figure 7-6

Amazon.com (AMZN)
Weekly

SPX

AMZN ——— 50-Day MA

Consolidating through time while the
general market is in correction mode.

Source: ycharts.com

Figure 7-7

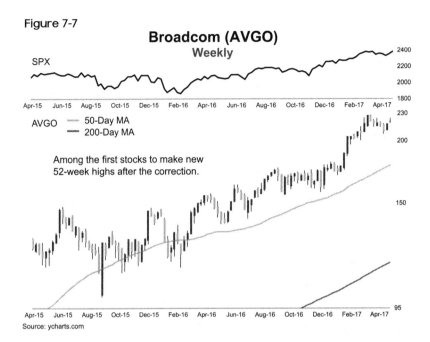

Broadcom (AVGO)
Weekly

SPX

AVGO — 50-Day MA
— 200-Day MA

Among the first stocks to make new
52-week highs after the correction.

Source: ycharts.com

Figure 7-8

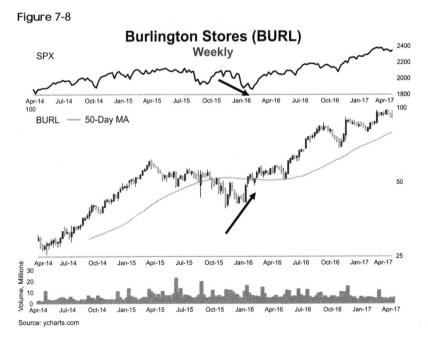

Burlington Stores (BURL)
Weekly

SPX

BURL — 50-Day MA

Source: ycharts.com

Figure 7-9

Chase (CCF)
Weekly

New 52-week highs during a
general market correction. Look
what happens when the market
starts to recover.

Source: ycharts.com

Figure 7-10

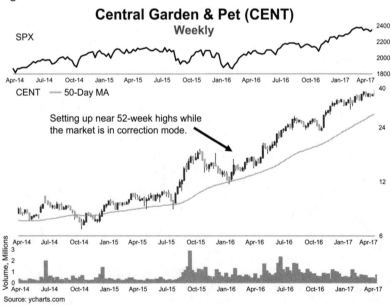

Central Garden & Pet (CENT)
Weekly

Setting up near 52-week highs while
the market is in correction mode.

Source: ycharts.com

Figure 7-11

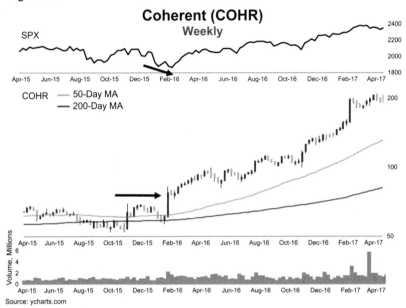

Source: ycharts.com

Figure 7-12

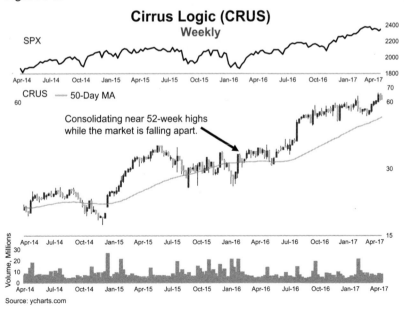

Source: ycharts.com

Figure 7-13

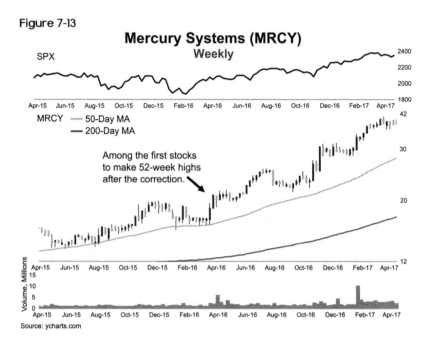

Mercury Systems (MRCY)
Weekly

Among the first stocks to make 52-week highs after the correction.

Source: ycharts.com

Figure 7-14

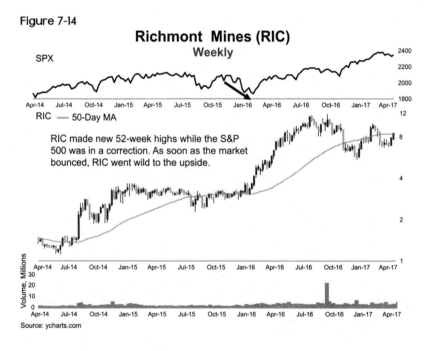

Richmont Mines (RIC)
Weekly

RIC made new 52-week highs while the S&P 500 was in a correction. As soon as the market bounced, RIC went wild to the upside.

Source: ycharts.com

When Is the Absolute Best Time to Buy Stocks?

You don't have to be in the market all the time, and you don't have to watch every uptick and every downtick.

In fact to do so would be very counterproductive and potentially dangerous for your returns. It's hard for professional money managers not to be active. Their clients almost demand it, as if being more active is positively correlated with higher returns. No, it's not. In fact it's often the opposite.

But being active is often interpreted as working hard. In markets it's more important to work smart, not hard. Less is more.

Most people will do incredibly well if they're active only four to five times a year and let their winners run long enough to make a difference. The best time to get aggressive and put money to work is right after a market correction.

The most money is made at the beginning and the end of a bull market, because no one believes the moves. At the beginning the fear of losing is stronger than the fear of missing out. At the end most people think it's too good to be true, and short-sellers are forced to cover their bets.

Warren Buffett likes to say that he's greedy when the majority is fearful and fearful when the majority is greedy.

Guess when people are most fearful: Right after the market in-dexes have had a quick 10% to15% correction and every post in the financial press is about doom and gloom.

Some of the biggest money-making opportunities in the stock market will come right after a big selloff. It's then that the risk is lowest and the potential rewards are highest. The best time to buy stocks is after a greater than 10% market correction. Sounds easy, but it is a lot harder in practice.

After a greater than 10% market correction most people are scared and think only about capital protection. The fear of losing is a lot bigger than the fear of missing out. Almost everyone hates stocks and is afraid of holding them for more than a few days.

Corrections often last long enough to condition most people to sell their winners quickly. As a result very few make any real money at the beginning stage of market recoveries.

It pays to be aggressive when others are afraid, but also keep in mind that, once in a while, a 10% correction turns into a 50% bear market. No one can know with any kind of certainty when the end of a correction and the beginning of a new rally is.

But here's a good rule of thumb.

The end of most market corrections is typically marked by breadth divergence. There's a divergence when an index makes new correction lows while a smaller number of its underlying stocks make new lows.

For example, let assume that the S&P 500 is down 10% (RSI) from its highs and there are 100 stocks that are making new 52-week lows. If the S&P 500 continues lower and its pullback reaches, let's say, 14% while the number of stocks making new 52-week lows decreases to 70, we have a divergence.

The existence of a divergence isn't enough for us to start buying heavily. Bottoms aren't formed by excessive selling. They're formed by strong buying.

You also need to see stocks that are breaking out to new 50-day or 52-week highs before you become more aggressive in your capital allocation.

Here are six annotated charts that illustrate these points.

Figure 7-15

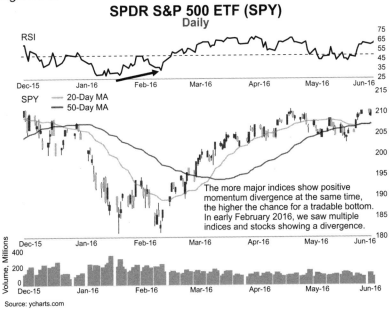

SPDR S&P 500 ETF (SPY)
Daily

The more major indices show positive momentum divergence at the same time, the higher the chance for a tradable bottom. In early February 2016, we saw multiple indices and stocks showing a divergence.

Source: ycharts.com

Figure 7-16

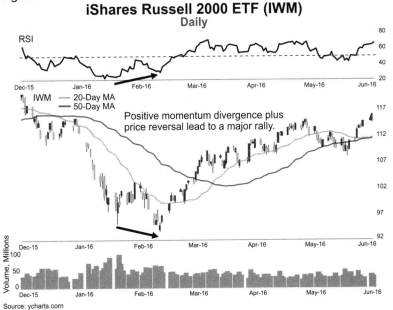

iShares Russell 2000 ETF (IWM)
Daily

Positive momentum divergence plus price reversal lead to a major rally.

Source: ycharts.com

Figure 7-17

Another positive momentum divergence. It occurs when a smaller number of NYSE stocks make new lows, which shows buyer's interest in select names. This reveals that the worst of the correction is possibly over and selling is not mindless anymore.

Source: ycharts.com

Figure 7-18

Source: ycharts.com

Figure 7-19

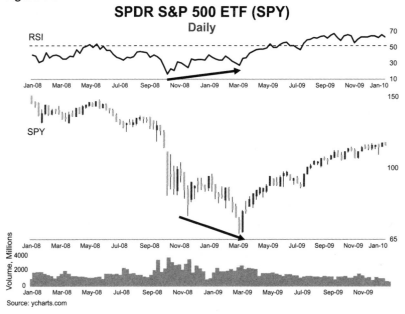

Source: ycharts.com

Figure 7-20

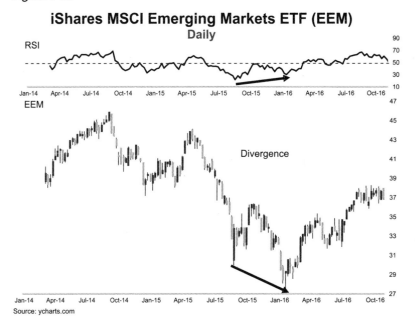

Source: ycharts.com

Now that we know when it's really a good time to buy, we should address the question of what to buy.

What are the best-performing stocks after a deep market correction?

The short answer is the ones that sold off the most during the correction.

The market tends to overreact during deep corrections and prices some stocks at extremely low valuations. The moment the market realizes that its pessimism is overblown, we could see some extreme moves in the worst-hit sectors during a correction.

And by "extreme" we mean 100% to 300% moves in two to eight weeks.

Another group worth our attention is growth stocks that held the best during the correction.

Growth stocks are usually high-beta names that get hit pretty hard in times of market panic. If any of them manage to hold above their 50-day moving average, build a new base, or even attempt to make a new 52-week high during the correction, they'll likely outperform significantly during any bounce attempt.

Note that we accentuate growth. During corrections it's normal to see low-beta, high-yield groups like utilities and consumer staples hold up better than the rest of the market. But they're not going to outperform during a market recovery.

Keep in mind that there are different types of corrections. In a garden-variety 5% to 10% pullback above a rising 200-day moving average, momentum stocks with the highest relative strength during the correction are likely to significantly outperform during a recovery.

After a deep, greater than 20% correction below a flat or declining 200-day moving average — and especially after a long bear market — many of the best performers will come from the most beaten down stocks that were priced for bankruptcy but managed to survive.

Some corrections turn into bear markets. They are rare, but they do happen. Bull markets reward risk-taking. But when the bear puts out honey, he's usually laying a trap. In bear markets you buy when the fear of losing is very high and you sell when the fear of missing out is very high.

As usual, it's easier said than done.

Figure 7-21

Mean Reversions

The recovery from a deep market correction is often quick and violent. Major indexes like the S&P 500 and the Nasdaq 100 will quickly reach technically oversold levels and stay there.

Correlations during the initial recovery stage are relatively high, so it makes all the sense in the world to use liquid, leveraged exchange-traded funds (ETFs). Direxion Small-Cap Bull 3X Shares, ProShares UltraPro QQQ, and ProShares UltraPro S&P 500 will do the job. This is also the time to start building a position in the inverse volatility exchange-traded note (ETN) VelocityShares Daily Inverse VIX Short-Term.

As the recovery process matures and major indexes like the S&P 500 and the Nasdaq Composite go back above their 50- and 200-day moving averages and act constructive once they get there, correlations will gradually dissipate and stock picking skills will start to matter again.

The best thing that could happen to an experienced trader is a 20%-plus market correction. The absolute best time to buy stocks is after a deep market correction.

The good news is you don't have to catch the absolute bottom. You can wait two to three weeks for a bottom to form before you start allocating money on the long side, and you could still make a lot of money.

Here are six annotated charts illustrating how hard-hit stocks, industries, and markets perform following corrections.

Figure 7-22

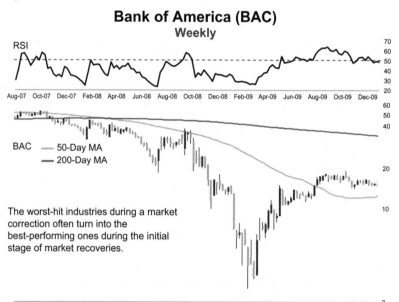

The worst-hit industries during a market correction often turn into the best-performing ones during the initial stage of market recoveries.

Source: ycharts.com

Figure 7-23

LendingTree (TREE)
Monthly

Big market corrections create opportunities to
generate angel investment-like returns with a lot less
risk, less work, and much higher rates of success.

TREE rose by more than 100 times
between early 2009 and 2015.

Source: ycharts.com

Figure 7-24

Direxion Daily Energy Bull 3x ETF (ERX)
Weekly

SPX

ERX
— 50-Day MA
— 200-Day MA

Look at the rally in the energy sector after the
market finally bottomed in 2016.

Source: ycharts.com

Figure 7-25

Direxion Daily Brazil Bull 3x ETF (BRZU)
Weekly

SPX

BRZU
— 50-Day MA
— 200-Day MA

Source: ycharts.com

Figure 7-26

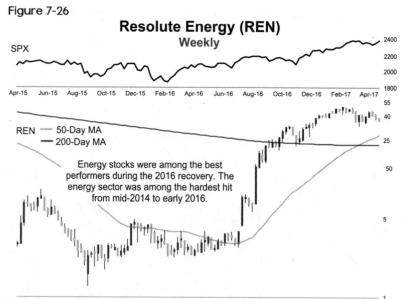

Resolute Energy (REN)
Weekly

SPX

REN   — 50-Day MA
        — 200-Day MA

Energy stocks were among the best
performers during the 2016 recovery. The
energy sector was among the hardest hit
from mid-2014 to early 2016.

Source: ycharts.com

Figure 7-27

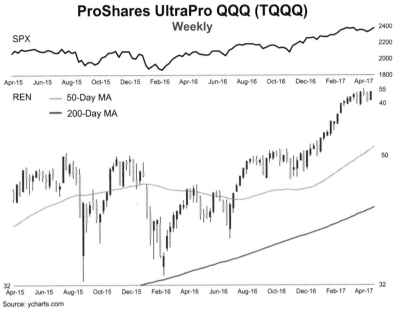

Source: ycharts.com

Relative Strength

The biggest market "secret" is that, from a long-term perspective, it's always been a "market of stocks" with many fat tails in both ends of the performance spectrum.

The first stocks to make new 52-week highs after a six- to 12-week correction are usually the ones that will outperform significantly over the next two to six months.

The silver lining of every correction is that it makes the spotting of future winners a lot easier. When markets correct, future leaders consolidate and form bases with incredible risk/reward prospects.

During corrections, it's important to pay attention to stocks that exhibit relative strength.

Relative strength is very simple to spot: Look for stocks that go sideways while the indexes drop significantly. During corrections, correlations often go to 1.00, meaning that most stocks move up and down together, regardless of their individual merits.

If a stock manages to hold its ground and consolidate through time or even make an attempt to make a new high, it's likely that institutions are accumulating shares.

Because of their size, many institutions prefer to buy on pullbacks and during market corrections, which provide liquidity to mask their accumulation. Once the pressure from the general market is removed, those stocks tend to outperform.

Relative strength is a powerful equity selection tool, but it could be very misleading at the beginning stages of a correction. In a real correction almost all stocks decline. Those that break out to new 52-week highs as the market averages start to deteriorate often quickly reverse lower.

As they say, from failed moves come fast moves.

The concept of relative strength adds a lot more value after the major indexes decline 7% to 10% or more.

If you remember only one principle from this book, it should be the concept of relative strength. Market pullbacks of at least 7% to 10% happen every single year.

During those corrections there are always stocks that consolidate sideways or try to make new 52-week highs while the averages plummet.

These are the stocks to which you want to pay special attention. These are the stocks you want to own heavily when the indexes bounce. These are the stocks that are very likely to become the next market leaders and go up 50% to 100% in the three to nine months after the correction.

These are the stocks that could make a real difference in your returns.

EIGHT

Sooner or Later Every Trend Ends

"It is not important whether we are right or wrong, but how much money we make when we are right and how much we lose, when we are wrong."

— George Soros

"We are in the business of making mistakes. The only difference between the winners and the losers is that the winners make small mistakes, while the losers make big mistakes."

— Ned Davis

Buy and Hold Is Not As Easy As It Sounds

You've probably heard some form of the following stories a thousand times.

Had you invested $10,000 in Starbucks at the day of its IPO in 1992, you'd be sitting on about $2.4 million as of mid-2017.

If you'd been brave enough to invest $10,000 in Priceline Group when it was a five-dollar stock in 2001, you'd be sitting on $1.8 million.

If you'd invested $10,000 in Cisco Systems in 1990, you'd have $6.7 million.

Hindsight bias makes investing seem a lot easier than it is.

Pointing out winners of the past could be a futile exercise if you don't realize the limitations of studying historical returns. What no one will tell you is that holding those stocks through their pullbacks was excruciatingly hard.

For each Starbucks, Priceline, and Cisco Systems there are hundreds of others that looked promising at the beginning stage of their price appreciation but failed to deliver positive long-term returns.

Any consistently successful investor will tell you that the secret behind accumulating wealth in the stock market is to cut your losers short and let your winners run. Anyone can buy a stock. Not everyone can hold a stock long enough to make a difference in his or her returns.

Holding is hard.

If you spend enough time investing, eventually you'll realize that the three smartest words in the field are ever say never. All big long-term winners go through deep pullbacks that challenge the conviction of even the most loyal shareholders. It's not easy to see your favorite stock go down 50% or 90%, no matter how much money you made in it in the past.

Here's a quick riddle about risk management.

Let's say you invest $10,000 in a stock with great growth potential. It goes up 1,000% in the next two years but then a bear market comes and hits all stocks. Your stock corrects 90%. How much is your investment worth after the correction? Exactly $10,000.

If you simply bought and held, you have as much money as you did when you began.

We don't know about you, but we don't think this return is very appealing.

Some trends last more than a decade and deliver percentage returns in the thousands. Some trends last only a few quarters and fizzle after a 200% to 300% move.

The truth is that, sooner or later, every trend ends. Some stocks manage to recover after a 50% pullback, make new 52-week highs, and offer good secondary buying opportunities. Many simply never recover from their big drawdowns or take a very, very long time to do so.

"Buy and hold forever" rarely works. The market graveyard is full of trends that last only a few quarters. The best-performing stocks in any given year are very volatile and not for the faint of heart.

Let's take a look at a few examples.

Yelp shares went from $20 to $100 in 2013. Then they declined 50%.

Figure 8-1

Yelp (YELP)
Weekly

Source: ycharts.com

GoPro shares went from $30 to $100 in about three months in 2014. Then they plunged 50%.

Figure 8-2

GoPro (GPRO)
Weekly

Source: ycharts.com

Pandora shares went from $10 to $37 in 2013 through early 2014. Then they dropped 70%.

Figure 8-3

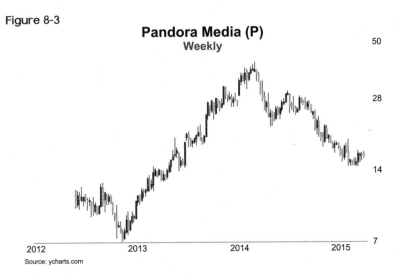

Bitauto Holdings shares went from $5 to $100 in two years. Then they dropped 50% in three months.

Figure 8-4

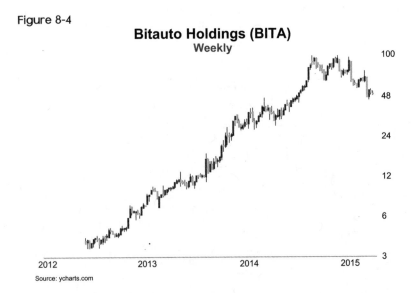

It's typical for story/momentum stocks to go up several hundred percentage points in a short period of time and then give back more than 50% of their move.

If we know that the trends of most high-growth momentum stocks last only several quarters and they experience tremendous drawdowns, why should we even bother with them as an asset class?

Because we could make a lot of money in them.

Their trends might end, but this doesn't mean that we have to give back most of the gains that they deliver.

Not every hot stock today will turn into a long-term winner. Most will turn out to be short-term fads. With some basic risk-management skills, you could still make a lot of money in them.

There are things that we know we know. There are things that we know we don't know. There are also things that we don't know we don't know. The biggest investment risks are usually in the third group.

We don't know which stocks will actually become huge long-term winners. We don't know how long a trend will last.

We know a good entry point from a risk/reward perspective. We know how much we risk, how much we allocate, where we'll add to our positions, and why we'll exit. We know which stocks have the potential to make a big move.

And that's all we need to know in order to consistently make money.

What are some of the things we don't know we don't know? Weird question, right?

For most people it's all about their empathy gap.

Empathy Gap

One of our favorite movie quotes ever is from *Batman Begins*: "It's not who you are underneath, it's what you do that defines you."

This quote describes perfectly the biggest obstacle for most investors and explains why there's a distance between desired and actual results.

An empathy gap — the difference between how you believe you will act under certain circumstances and how you actually act when the time comes — is the main cause behind most trading and investing mistakes.

Do you think you'll remain calm in the face of a 50% decline in one or several of your holdings and you'll ride them back to new all-time highs? Think again.

Most people will give up and sell in the face of such big losses. You have to plan for your inherent human weaknesses. You need to have a clear strategy that will your protect profits and confidence.

Maybe Your Goal Shouldn't Be to Find the Next Apple

Maybe your goal shouldn't be to find stocks that will go up 2,000% in 20 years.

Warren Buffett likes to marry his stocks and ride them through good and bad 'til death do them part. His approach is not for everyone.

A much better approach for you might be to aim at stocks that could go up 100% to 500% in six to 24 months and sell them as they violate their uptrends.

Finding stocks that have the potential to be the next Apple is easy only in hindsight. The truth is that no one can know for sure.

If you could go back in time and tell Steve Jobs and Tim Cook how successful Apple would become, they'd probably think you were crazy. Even they had no idea in the early 2000s.

Very few of today's leaders will turn into the next Apple. The few that do will have incredibly volatile paths along the way. Riding those trends through their inevitable greater than 50% drawdowns will make holding them pretty much impossible for most people.

The good news is that there will be thousands of mini-Apples in your life as an investor, thousands of stocks that will go up 100% to 200% in a year or two. Anyone could catch 10 or 20 of them.

The Magic of Compounding

Five-thousand dollars invested in Home Depot when it went public in 1981 is now worth about $30 million.

Turning $5,000 into $30 million over 35 years means that Home Depot compounded at an average annual rate of a little more than 28%.

That's very, very rare. Let's compare Home Depot's return to some of the best-performing stocks of all time:

- $5,000 invested in Microsoft in 1986 is worth about $4.85 million.

- $5,000 invested in Walmart in 1975 is worth about 29 million.

- $5,000 invested in Applied Materials in 1975 is worth about $22 million.

Amazon stock's compounding is even more impressive. Amazon has been public for 20 years. An investment in the online shopping behemoth at the time of its 1997 IPO is worth about $2.6 million today. Amazon has generated an average annual return of 37% per year for 20 years. It'd be really challenging for Bezos & Company to sustain that pace of growth for the next decade or so.

Finding a stock that has the potential to compound at 28% annually for 35 years is close to impossible, and probably, it won't be repeated ever again. Indeed, simply holding such a stock for 35 years might be even harder.

What if, instead of finding a stock that can compound annually at 28% for 35 years, you find a stock that can go up 28% this year? And then you repeat the exercise every year for 35 years, one stock at a time?

Or maybe we find five or 10 stocks at a time.

It won't be easy. But it's also a lot more manageable, because in any given year there are hundreds, even thousands, of stocks that go up more than 30% for the year.

Very few achieve that return year after year. But you don't need to own them every year. Compounding can be magical.

Why Trends End

Some trends last several months and others several years, but eventually they all end. This is not an opinion. It's a fact.

The goal of investing is to keep your profits when the inevitable correction comes.

Trends end when expectations change. Expectations could change for various reasons. Here are three major ones.

The first such catalyst is weakness in the general market.

All stocks are price-cyclical. A company could triple its earnings and still lose 50% of its market cap in a bear market. Sentiment trumps fundamentals from a short-term perspective.

Violent market corrections often lead to panic-selling. During periods of forced liquidations and redemptions, all stocks suffer. Forced liquidation means "get me out at any price." Even the stocks of the most solid businesses suffer in such periods.

Second, no company can sustain high expectations forever.

Anything priced for perfection eventually disappoints. The cause for a letdown could be missing earnings expectations, but this isn't always the case. The stock market is forward-looking, and it discounts proactively.

That means price trends often start and end before earnings growth trends reverse.

Many trends have good fundamental basis. They're based on rational expectations. The market is forward-looking, but it's constantly looking for feedback, in terms of positive growth data. If it doesn't receive it, it reevaluates its initial thesis and starts to correct.

A good story can get you only so far.

At some point people wake up from their dreams. They sober up and realize that not only have they discounted a future that's never going to materialize (at least not soon) but they also could actually lose money if they keep holding their position.

Many smart people like to take partial profits on strength. At some point their supply overwhelms the underlying demand, which causes a huge counter-trend range expansion. There comes a big down day or week.

All of a sudden more people realize that they're not untouchable and that buying shouldn't be mindless.

The fear of losing gradually overwhelms the fear of missing out.

Trends last because the market tends to over-discount identified risks and opportunities, until one day it realizes that the perception and the reality are miles away and there's no chance of them aligning anytime soon.

Corrections happen not necessarily because the market is discounting some future event. Sometimes they happen because the market is correcting a previously incorrect view.

Then there's the fact that valuation eventually matters.

Sometimes the market will give the benefit of the doubt to a company with great growth potential, and it will discount a bright future. But not all companies live up to the expectations.

At some point the market will realize it's been wrong all along, and it will correct itself. Investors will wake up from their sweet dreams, and suddenly the fear of losing will trump the fear of missing out.

When this happens, look out below.

When growth stocks are in an uptrend valuation doesn't matter. The people who invest in them don't buy or sell for valuation reasons. It's all about sentiment, expectations, and earnings per share and sales growth.

Some short-sellers fade growth names on valuation reasons alone, but they could be wrong for 300% before they're right for a 50% pullback.

Valuation matters when market mood shifts from complacency and euphoria to doom and gloom.

One of the ways to gauge sentiment shift is to watch the market's reaction to earnings reports.

When the market reacts poorly to what appears to be "good news" on the surface, consider it a major sign that the trend might be over or at least a reminder that the easy money in the trend has already been made.

Valuation matters once an uptrend is broken and a stock starts to slide.

A stock could go up 500% in a year and then lose 50% of it in a couple months. A correction usually comes a lot slower than everyone anticipates, and when it happens it develops a lot faster than anyone expects.

Growth stocks often take the stairwell up and an elevator down. The decline is more furious, because there is no one to support them on the way down. When a momentum stock appreciates, it climbs a constant wall of worry. Skepticism slowly dissipates until that stock accelerates its momentum and forces all short sellers to cover their bets.

In this stage a typical momentum stock will go parabolic. It could run 50% in a couple weeks or less.

Such momentum spikes are used by smart investors and institutions to unload some or all of their shares. Institutions need liquidity in order to establish large enough positions. This is why they prefer to buy individual stocks on pullbacks or during general market corrections that send all stocks lower. Institutions also need liquidity in order to sell their large positions.

That liquidity often comes from short-sellers who receive margin calls and are forced to cover their bets and late-comers who chase and enter a momentum stock very late in its price cycle, for example after it's appreciated 300% in the past year and it's very extended from its latest technical base.

In this case the fear of missing out trumps the fear of losing.

Why do most momentum stocks decline so much after they peak? Because there's no one to support them.

Momentum investors and trend-followers who bought on the way up are either out or short. Value investors don't even touch those stocks. The market is very likely to overreact to the downside if it had overreacted to the upside before.

It's like pushing a swing: The stronger you push in one direction, the stronger it comes back to you.

Finally, sometimes we see an increase in the supply of a company's stock.

Many companies use their stock as a currency. They could print as much as they want, and many do, to pay their employees, for example, and management and to acquire competitors. This is why most companies' shares outstanding increase over time.

If the company's management doesn't screw it up, Wall Street will. Wall Street is a tireless printing press and a sophisticated distribution and marketing machine. It's in the business of printing stocks that are in demand by the market.

When a company is hot, two things happen: management calls a banker or a banker calls management. If the company is already public the call is for a potential secondary offering. If the company is still private the call is for an IPO.

More shares in one stock category impacts negatively the supply/demand dynamics. Overstuffing the IPO pipeline is very similar to creating excess capacity. Eventually it puts downward pressure on prices.

Wall Street's job is to print as much paper to satisfy the most people at exactly the wrong time. All trends end the same way: too many shares distributed to far too many people.

As investors we have to focus on the positive. Yes, all trends end., But while they last they could deliver substantial returns.

We just have to know when to enter and when to exit.

The Three Pillars of Risk Management

Proper equity selection, which includes timing, is the first pillar of risk management. Safety is derived from proper timing. Timing isn't everything, but it is of crucial importance.

We aim to own stocks with potential for substantial and quick price appreciation. We also aim to enter them at a spot that will put us at an immediate profit, which will allow us to go through normal market pullbacks.

If we end up being wrong, it will allow us to exit at a small, manageable loss.

The second pillar is to have an exit strategy, and that means knowing when to take a loss and when to take profits.

The final pillar is diversification and position sizing.

Let's go in-depth on the pillars, one by one.

Pillar One: Equity Selection

The father of value investing, Benjamin Graham, will tell you to look for stocks with margins of safety — that is, stocks that are worth more when liquidated than they're currently priced in the market.

The theory of "margin of safety" is simply not applicable for most of today's markets. It was created during the Great Depression, when the market was full of stocks trading below their liquid assets' market price. Nowadays this rarely happens, if ever.

Graham's favorite student, Warren Buffett, advises us to look for "sustainable advantage." What would be the damage to your business if someone invested $1 billion to create competition? If the damage is likely to be minor, it's likely a good business to own for the long term.

Our own definition of "safety" is very different.

We believe that safety is derived more from the proper timing of our entries and exits than from the quality of the underlying company.

All stocks are price-cyclical. The stock prices of the strongest U.S. corporations have experienced greater than 50% drawdowns during big market corrections. Most people can't stomach such drawdowns, and they'll probably sell when they get scared, which often happens near the lows.

Buffett's business partner, Charlie Munger, says that if you're unable to stomach a 50% drawdown in your investment holdings, you're probably not fit to take advantage of the rewards that long-term investing brings.

There has to be a different way to approach this issue.

First of all, not all stocks will eventually come back to their highs, or it might take a very long time for them to do so.

Second of all, if you are a small individual investor, there's no reason to let your capital holdings depreciate 50%. When you incur a 50% loss, you'll need a 100% gain just to break even. This is a lot of work. Why not work smarter rather than harder?

Why not cut your losses when they're small (up to 10%) and, in the process, protect your confidence?

Protecting your confidence during market correction is just as important as protecting your capital. If you lose your confidence due to a large number of oversized losses, you won't be in the right psychological state to take advantage of a market rally when it arrives. This would be a terrible thing to happen.

Our equity selection takes the following criteria into account, in order of importance.

1. A breakout to new 50-day high or 52-week high from a great technical base.

   • A breakout helps our timing immensely. It assures that we put money to work in a fast-moving asset. Opportunity cost is important to us. We'd like to allocate money to stocks that are likely to move in our favor immediately after our entry. If the general market is strong, we might buy in expectation of a breakout.

   • A great technical base clearly defines our stop. If this level is breached, we're wrong. We accept it, take our losses, and hunt for other stocks. There are no hard feelings. There are plenty of fish in the sea.

2. It has catalysts we understand. It either belongs to a currently hot industry or it has strong earnings and sales growth — even better if it has both.

Pillar Two: Exit Strategy: When to Take Profits and How to Keep Losses Small

If you don't know why you buy a stock, you won't know where to exit. If price action is the reason for your purchase, price action should be the reason to sell.

What are some of the reasons to take partial profits or to entirely liquidate a position?

Poor Reaction to Good News

The market is forward-looking, because everyone tries to be one move ahead of the rest. Prices change when expectations change. By the time expectations are confirmed or disconfirmed by facts (news or earnings reports), most of the move might be already over.

If you're waiting for the comfort of good news to buy or the shock of bad news to tell you when to exit, you'll always be behind the curve in the investing game.

When a stock reacts negatively to what appears to be a good earnings report on the surface, take note. There's a major change in sentiment, which often puts an end to the underlying price trend.

Price trends often start and end before earnings trends. Take, for example, the case of Cirrus Logic, which is a major supplier to Apple.

When Cirrus destroyed earnings estimates in November 2012, many people were shocked to see the market reaction — a gap down from $41 to $37. At the time the gap was perceived as a buying opportunity by many who cited the spectacular earnings growth. By June 2013, Cirrus was trading near $17 per share.

Surprises often follow the direction of the established trend, until the end. Knowing when that elusive end could be is extremely useful.

Poor reaction to what's perceived to be a good earnings report is usually one of the first signs that the price trend is over, and, because price is the only thing that pays us, it's the main trend to which we should pay attention.

Figure 8-5

Cirrus Logic (CRUS)
Weekly

Crushes earnings estimates

Reports record growth

Market sells the good news

Poor reaction to good news is a
sign of major changes in sentiment.

Mar-12   May-12   Jul-12   Sep-12   Nov-12   Jan-13   Mar-13   May-13   Jul-13

Source: ycharts.com

Distribution

George Soros says that short-term volatility tends to rise at turning points. Look for sudden high-volume, large range-expansion daily or weekly moves against the established trend.

For example, a stock that declines 5% in a day above its average daily volume is probably under distribution.

We have two simple definitions for distribution:

- Institutional selling. Institutions are taking profits or need capital to allocate it to other assets. Institutional money is not necessarily the smartest money, but its size has the ability to move stocks —to start and to end trends. It's unwise not to pay attention to it.

- Transfer of ownership. This is, often the case of ownership shifting from strong to weak hands, from people who are looking to lock in profits in extended names to people who are chasing out of greed and fear of missing out. Why do we call the buyers here weak hands? Because when you chase and buy a stock that's too extended from its late technical base, you put yourself in a very vulnerable position. High-growth momentum stocks don't go up every day. They experience normal pullbacks along their uptrend. Not if but when such pullback happens, people who chased will be left under water. What do people who are in a losing position often do? They hope to sell at break-even prices. Even if their stock bounces, it will add to their selling pressure, which is likely to accelerate its downtrend.

When distribution days start to be frequent, chasing isn't so mindless anymore. Most people realize that they could actually lose money, which changes their behavior entirely. The fear of losing starts to trump the fear of missing out.

Figure 8-6

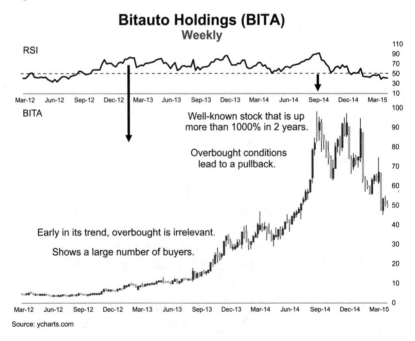

Source: ycharts.com

Figure 8-7

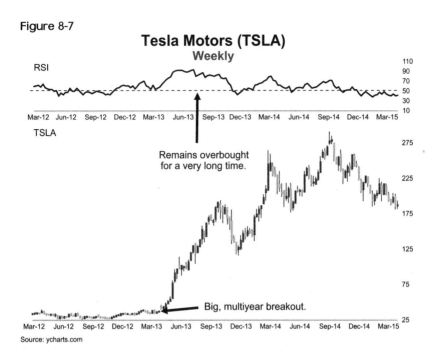

Source: ycharts.com

Reaching Severely Overbought Levels (When Weekly RSI Goes Above 80)

Reaching those levels is usually a good spot to take partial profits. "RSI" (or "relative strength indicator") is a simple technical tool, offered by every charting platform.

The technical term "overbought" basically means "acceleration in buying to levels that might not be sustainable for too long."

What could possibly be wrong about an overwhelming number of buyers?

It might be an indication that there's no one left to buy. Some institutions need the liquidity that new highs provide in order to exit a big position.

Using a weekly RSI above 80 is a good rule of thumb, but it's not perfect. There are stocks that remain overbought for a very long time and go up 100% to 200% after hitting that level. It's rare, but it happens.

In 2013 Tesla Motors went from $55 to $200 while its weekly RSI stayed above 80. The hottest stocks of each year often don't care about overbought conditions.

Under overbought conditions, you need to look at everything in context. Those conditions could resolve through time consolidation or through a price pullback.

Here are "context questions" to consider.

- Is it a fresh breakout from a humongous base? Have earnings just accelerated? In this case an overbought condition is likely to be the beginning of a powerful new trend, not the end.

- Is the stock already up more than 800% in the past three years? Do most analysts have a "buy" rating on the stock? Is the institutional ownership above 90%? Are the CEO and the company featured on the cover of magazines, the front page of newspapers, and website landing pages? In this case a severely overbought condition is a good reason for partial profit-taking.

Figure 8-8

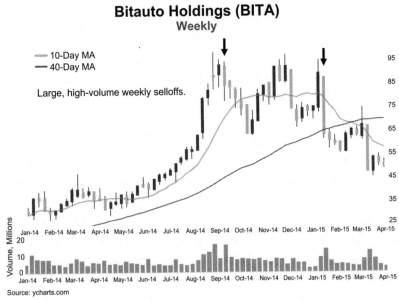

Source: ycharts.com

Figure 8-9

Yelp (YELP)
Weekly

When a Trend Is Over

This is usually obvious only in hindsight. There's no perfect exit strategy, but having one is better than not having one. You have to accept that you're not going to catch the entire move. That's OK. You don't have to.

The following is a good rule of thumb. Exit when there is:

- A lower low, a close below the most recent time consolidation
- A new 50-day low
- The price closes below the 100-day moving average
- The price closes below the 50-week moving average

When Your Stop Loss Is Hit

Stops should be placed at a level that invalidates our investing or trading thesis. This usually means a close below the most recent sideways consolidation.

If Shakespeare were alive today, he'd probably be a really good investor:

I always feel happy. Do you know why? Because I don't expect anything from anyone. Expectations always hurt.

Substitute "my stocks" for "anyone" and you get good market wisdom to live by:

I always feel happy. Do you know why? Because I don't expect anything from my stocks. Expectations always hurt.

We sure would like new entries to be profitable. But we have to accept the fact that we're not going to be right every time. If we're not right every time, then it's important to keep our losses to a minimum.

There are times when everything will look perfect, and you'll pull the trigger and still be wrong. Don't worry about it. It happens.

Being wrong is not a choice. Staying wrong is.

We try to stay longer with the stocks that make us happy — the stocks that make us money. We try to kick the stocks that make us sad — the ones that make us lose money.

We don't expect to catch big winners every time. We definitely expect to be wrong on some occasions. But we always know how much we have at risk, and so should you. Never let one investment decide your destiny.

Most people simply can't believe that a market leader could decline 50% or even more than 80% from its high, despite the fact that financial history is full of examples of old leaders having substantial pullbacks.

Remember the three smartest words in the field: Never say never. All big winners, without exception, experience a deep pullback at one point of their price cycle. We're talking declines of 40%, 50%, or more.

Some of those stocks recover and offer good secondary buying opportunities. But many never recover. These are the ones from which we have to protect our portfolio and our confidence.

The opportunity cost of sticking to your losers is not being able to redeploy that cash to new winners. Sure, they might end up recovering, but in the meantime there will probably be stocks that will do a lot better.

The market is an opportunity machine, and it will deliver a lot of fat pitches in your trading career. You just have to make sure you're in a position to take advantage of them.

You do that by cutting your losses, limiting your drawdown, and protecting your capital and your confidence.

Pillar Three: Diversification and Position Sizing

They say that diversification is the only free lunch. They also say that diversification protects wealth, and concentration could help to create it.

What's your approach to diversification? Do you like to bet big and put all your eggs in one basket, or do you prefer to play it safe and spread the risk?

Entrepreneurs put all their money, time, and social capital (reputation) in one place. Not all succeed, but those who do enjoy huge payback. Those who don't make it the first time just find a job to pay the bills before pursuing another idea.

Venture capitalists (people who invest in entrepreneurs and their ideas) are much more conservative. On the surface, venture capitalists might look like riverboat gamblers who invest in startups without defined product or revenue, run by fearless kids with zero experience.

In reality, VCs never put all their money in one idea for one simple reason: There are no sure things.

Entrepreneurs and venture capitalists have direct influence on the success of their efforts. There is no guarantee, but they are more or less in control of their own destiny.

Public investors, on the other side, have very little control over how a company operates or how the rest of the market will decide to price it. You could speculate, based on experience and forward-looking thinking, where a stock is likely to go. But you could never be 100% sure it'll happen.

No one knows the future, which means that some form of diversification makes sense for you.

One great stock idea could change your life if you hold it long enough to make a difference. But you should always have more than one good stock idea, because one could go wrong for various unforeseeable reasons.

Don't let one stock wreck the wonders of the market for you. It's totally normal and acceptable to be wrong. You just have to make sure that you live to invest another day.

The most important market rule is to always hold yourself accountable for your investments. It's fine to borrow other people's ideas. You don't have to be first in order to make money in the stock market, but you should never transfer responsibility and point fingers. You can't blame anyone — not insiders, not the CEO, not dark pools, and not institutions.

You need several ideas, but how many exactly?

What do Warren Buffett, David Tepper, George Soros, and Stanley Druckenmiller have in common, other than some of the best long-term track records in money management? They like to make concentrated bets. Their approach is not for the faint of heart. They might not be diversified, but they're using other means for protection — either time is on their side or they have a firm stop loss in sight.

Warren Buffett says that "diversification is a protection against ignorance". This is why he advises most non-professionals to own well-diversified, low-fee index funds such as the SPDR S&P 500 ETF or the PowerShares QQQ Trust.

On the other side, professional investors should limit their holdings to six names so they can get to know them better.

Buffett's approach is to buy great businesses at reasonable valuations. He can wait 20 years for a business to eventually recover. It usually takes a lot less time. "Time is a friend of the good business," he notes, "and enemy of the mediocre business."

Tepper is a buyer of debt and equity of distressed companies during market crashes. He knows that he can be early, but his size requires him to be early:

For better or worse we're a herd leader. We're at the front of the pack, we are one of the first movers. First movers are interesting, you get to the good grass first, or sometimes the lion eats you.

We're value-oriented and performance-based like a lot of funds. But I think what differentiates us is that we're not afraid of the downside of different situations when we've done the analysis. Some other people are very afraid of losing money, which keeps them from making money.

Druckenmiller believes diversification is one of the most misguided concepts they teach in business schools. He likes to put all of his eggs into one basket and watch that basket carefully.

Soros is convinced that when you have a high conviction on a trade, you have to go for the jugular. It takes a lot of courage to ride a profit with a huge leverage. According to Soros, "You cannot own enough, when you are right."

Soros is also a really good loss-taker who doesn't lose his confidence because of short-term results. He understands that it doesn't matter if you're right or wrong on a trade. What matters how much money you make when you're right and how much you lose when you're wrong. You can be right only 30% of the time and still end up doing very well.

Soros and Druckenmiller make concentrated bets only when certain conditions align:

- They always have an exit strategy. When they made their famous bet against the British pound, they knew exactly how much they could lose — their entire year-to-date gain of 12%.

- They say that the right conditions to make a concentrated bet happen only once or twice a year. Not everyone is able to recognize those conditions. Proper timing is everything when you trade big. A good entry point allows you to go through normal market reactions. An amazing entry point allows to use a tighter stop-loss and, therefore, to take on a bigger position size.

- They're aggressive only when they earn the right to be aggressive. If they manage to start the year with large gains, they're more willing to press their luck and look for home runs via concentrated bets.

We believe that there is a middle ground between indexing and highly concentrated bets that fits better the lifestyle and goals of most of us. Owning six to −12 stocks by allocating 10% to 20% of your capital to each is a good alternative.

When you allocate 20% of your capital to one idea and your stop-loss is 10% below your entry, the most you could lose would be 2% of your capital. Can you live with that? If not you might want to use a smaller position size. If that idea doubles the contribution to your total capital would be 20%.

NINE

The Stock Market Is an Opportunity Machine

"The stock market is not the kind of game in which one party loses what another wins. It is the kind of game in which, over certain periods of time, nearly everyone may win, or nearly everyone may lose."

— James Grant

Nothing Is Guaranteed to Anyone

Warren Buffett is a huge fan of Coca-Cola, not only as an investor but also as a consumer. Here's a story he told at the University of Florida in 1998:

Coca-Cola IPO'd in 1919 for $40. A year later, it was $19. You can always find a few reasons why that was not a good time to buy it, but if you bought one share at $40 and reinvested the dividends, you would have $5 million today. This factor overrides everything — all macro concerns you could have. There is never a perfect time to buy a great business; there is always a reason to worry, but you should also know when it is wise to worry at all. For things that are unimportant or unknown, you should not worry. If you are right about the business, you will make a lot of money over time.

Buffett also added that if he had to put all his money in one stock for the next 20 years, he definitely wouldn't mind if it were Coca-Cola.

Well, for the 19 years after his speech the capital gain of Coca-Cola was 11% (not including dividends). Not 11% per year, but 11% for the entire period.

The S&P 500 returned 113% for the same time (not including dividends). If we include dividends, the total return of the S&P 500 since 1998 is 202%, or about 6% annualized. The total return of Coca-Cola (with reinvested dividends) was 122%.

Proper market-timing matters, regardless of the virtues of the underlying company. Just because a business has strong brands and pricing power doesn't necessarily make it a great investment.

There are no sure things in the market. Nothing is guaranteed to anyone.

Buffett jokes that he prefers simple businesses that could be run by idiots because, sooner or later they will be. He hates uncertainty and wants to invest in companies that are likely to earn a lot more 10 years from now. He loves strong brands, because they have high mind-share and pricing power.

Figure 9-1

Buffett advises long-term investors to not choose stocks based on the impact their industry will have on society but based on how durable their competitive advantage is.

The truth is that very few companies can sustain their competitive advantage for a very long time. And if they do the market often prices that in their stocks today, so their future return is hardly a big surprise.

Companies that are well-known and easily predictable tend to deliver average market returns, at best — as was the case with Coca-Cola over the past 19 years.

There Are Different Types of Trends

In markets, and in life, there are trends that last only a year, and there are trends that last several decades. You could make a lot of money in both types of trends if you learn how to properly time your exits and entries.

Financial history is full of examples of stocks that went up 300%, 500%, or 1,000% in a few quarters and then gave most of it back for various reasons.

Earnings growth naturally slowed down, competition erased margins, investors' expectations about the future of the stocks declined significantly, the general market went into correction, etc.

BlackBerry went from $2 to $150 in five years, and then it dropped 95% in the following four years.

Figure 9-2

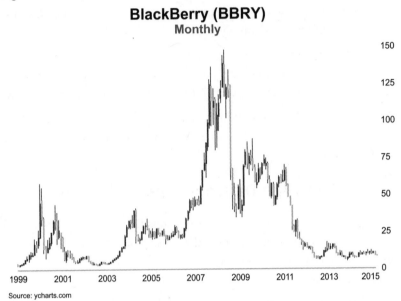

BlackBerry (BBRY)
Monthly

Source: ycharts.com

Just because we don't know if a company can sustain its competitive advantage for more than a few years or remain a market leader, should we miss on a several-hundred or even several-thousand percent return?

From 2003 to 2008 U.S. Steel Corp. went from $10 to $180. Over the next year it gave back almost everything, and it went back to $20.

Figure 9-3

U.S. Steel Group (X)
Monthly

Source: ycharts.com

In early 2015 U.S. Steel was trading below its IPO price from 1991, providing 24 years of nothing for those that just bought and held on (and hoped).

You don't need to a ride a trend for 10 years in order to make a difference in your returns. There are plenty of decent trends that last only a year or two and deliver substantial profits for those who have an exit strategy.

Timing Matters

Netflix has been one of the craziest stocks in the past decade. There were four distinct stages (all prices are before its 7-for-1 stock split):

- From 2009 to mid-2011 it went from $30 to $300.

- It tanked to $60 in four short months, constituting an 80% drop in a little over a quarter.

- It spent about a year of going nowhere, frustrating both bulls and bears, eventually reaching the ultimate level of neglect and indifference. It was even kicked out of the Nasdaq 100 near the end of 2012, when it was a $90 stock.

- In January 2013 it emerged to new 52-week highs and went up to $500 per share.

Figure 9-4

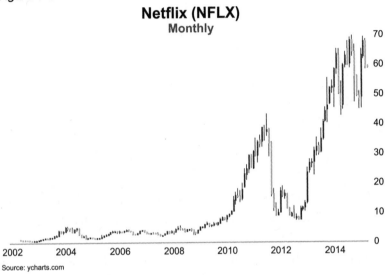

Netflix (NFLX)
Monthly

Source: ycharts.com

How is it possible for a stock to fluctuate so much inside four years? Would you call this "efficient"?

Netflix is the poster child for inefficient markets. The company can't be valued properly as it grows, shrinks, and grows, so you have surprises.

How can you say that timing doesn't matter for such a stock — or, for that matter, for any stock?

The only constants in financial markets are change and uncertainty. Not only business environments change, but also people's perceptions of stocks change.

Keurig Green Mountain went from making a new all-time high at $10 in March 2009 to $115 in September 2011. Then it pulled back. By the summer of 2012, it was trading under $20. In early 2015, it was back above $125. And now, as of mid-2017, it's just above $90.

Emerge Energy Services went from $17 to $145 in less than two years. Then it dropped all the way down to $4 per share in the next two years. It went back up to $24, only to collapse back to $12 again.

Figure 9-5

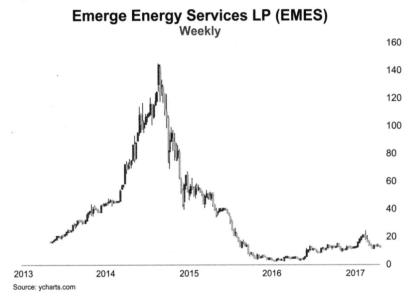

Emerge Energy Services LP (EMES)
Weekly

Source: ycharts.com

Earnings growth and valuation drives prices from a long-term perspective. Sentiment and confidence are what matter the most in the short term, and they often produce results that seem irrational and extreme.

"Short term" could be anywhere from several weeks to a couple years. It's the way the market works. You can do nothing. You can even complain about it.

Or you can learn the rules of the market game and use that knowledge to build wealth.

Trends come and go. Some last only a few quarters. Others last several years. We don't know how long a trend is going to last, but we don't need to in order to benefit from it.

Proper equity selection is of utmost importance. The most important part of equity selection is timing.

Is Timing Equally Important If You Invest in Well-diversified Indexes?

Some argue that timing is irrelevant when it comes to dollar-cost averaging in low-fee indexes.

Tell that to Japanese investors. Between 1970 and 1981, Japanese stocks returned an average of 21% annually. To put things in perspective, $10,000 invested in the Nikkei in 1970 was worth $450,000 by 1989.

Then everything turned upside down and, in the next 25 years, the Nikkei's average annual performance dropped to negative 2%. Here's some more perspective: $10,000 invested in the Nikkei in 1990 was worth about $6,000 by the end of 2014.

Dollar-cost averaging in a single index doesn't seem like such a sure bet, does it?

Figure 9-6

Nikkei 225
Monthly

Source: St. Louis Federal Reserve

You don't need to study Japan to understand the cyclicality in overall market returns. What happened in Japan has happened in many other capital markets.

They say a picture is worth a thousand words. Consider the following graphs, showing returns for the S&P 500 (or its equivalent at the time) since 1903. Strong periods lasted 10 to 15 years on average, and then they were followed by periods of disappointing results.

Figure 9-7

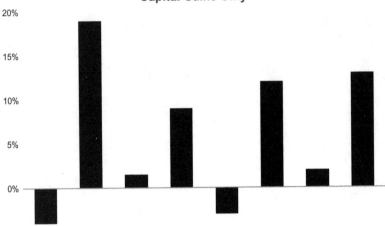

Figure 9-8

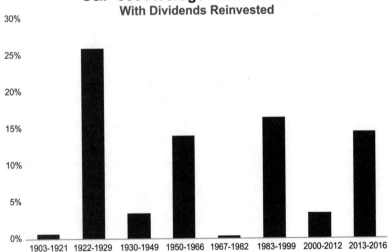

Figure 9-9

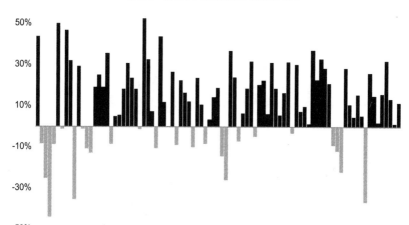

S&P 500 Annual Return

Source: http://pages.stern.nyu.edu/~adamodar/New_Home_Page/datafile/histretSP.html

As you can see in these charts, there are no guarantees in the stock market.

Periods of extremely strong returns are followed by periods of underwhelming performance. It took 13 years and two bear markets for the S&P 500 to substantially surpass its levels from the dot-com boom.

It cleared new all-time highs in 2013, and it hasn't looked back since then.

The big question is, what's next?

Why the Next 10 Years Will Be a Stock-Pickers' Market

In late 1999 Warren Buffet told the world that the next 17 years will be a lot more challenging for the stock market than the previous 17 years, which had delivered record gains. Buffett added that he would be really surprised if the stock market achieved a return higher than nominal GDP growth.

There were only four ways to achieve higher returns:

- If interest rates dropped significantly. They did, from 6% to under 3%.

- If corporate earnings increased their cut of GDP. They did, from 6% to 9%.

- If valuation went even higher than it was. It was already too stretched in 1999, so it was normal to see some form of mean-reversion there.

- If you're a great stock picker.

Buffett's educated guess turned out to be spot on. Ten years later (by 2009), the S&P 500 had dropped 30%. Between 1999 and 2016, the S&P 500 nominal return (not including dividends) was 52%. If we adjust for reinvested dividends, then the S&P 500's return is 116%.

Nominal GDP growth was 92% for the same period.

Figure 9-10

Historic U.S. 10-Year Treasury Yield

Source: Federal Reserve

Figure 9-11

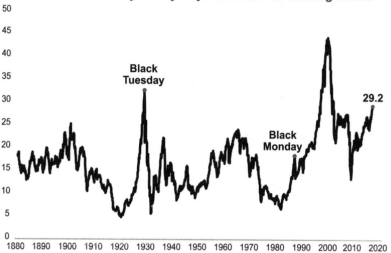

Present Stock Valuation Approaching 1929 Peak
Shiller's 10-Year Cyclically-Adjusted Price-to-Earnings Ratio

Source: http://www.econ.yale.edu/~shiller/data.htm

Figure 9-12

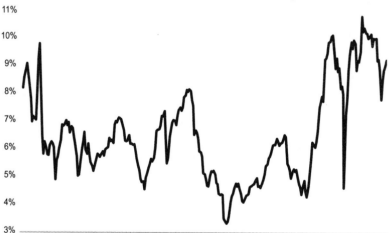

U.S. Corporate Profits as a Percentage of GDP

Source: St. Louis Federal Reserve

Let's take a look at the current standing of the three major factors (as of the spring of 2017) that could drive long-term profits for the stock market in general.

Interest rates are still near historical lows, but they have been rising steadily over the past year. The odds are that they'll continue to edge higher, which will put negative pressure on stocks as an asset class.

Corporate profits as a percentage of GDP are at record highs near 9%. Financial history and logic say that their cut of GDP is not likely to increase much from those levels — unless there's a substantial cut in corporate taxes, which is one of the main promises of the Trump administration.

If it happens, this would have a substantially positive impact on stocks in general.

Valuations are a little stretched, but are still nowhere near 2000's levels. Stocks could get a boost here, but we wouldn't bet on it.

Assuming that, on a net basis, these three factors won't have a negative impact on stocks (they could easily do so), the total market performance in the next 10 years will depend only on two other elements:

- Nominal GDP growth. If we assume about 4% to 5% nominal growth (which is very optimistic given the numbers over the past 20 years) and 2% dividends, the best-case scenario is about 6% to 7% average annual total market returns, which isn't too bad.

- Your stock-picking skills. Anything above or below that 6% to 7% annual average will depend on your ability to pick stocks and allocate to different asset classes.

The numbers suggest we're likely headed for another challenging decade for stock market investors. This is a challenge. It's also an opportunity.

The period between 2000 and 2010 brought a lot of turbulence. We had two "once-in-a-hundred-years" storms: the big correction in early 2000, when the Nasdaq Composite declined 80%, and 2008-09, when the S&P 500 suffered a 57% plunge.

The very same decade also brought us epic bull markets in commodities and emerging markets, monstrous trends in consumer discretionary that brought us Monster Beverage and Chipotle, and the emergence of technology names like Apple, Google, BlackBerry, and Netflix.

These are just a few of the huge multiyear moves that happened during this "lost decade."

Even if the next 10 years turn out to be just as volatile and crazy as the first decade of the 21st century, and even if the major equity indexes deliver negative returns for the decade and we go through several humongous corrections, there will be plenty of opportunities for shrewd traders and investors to consistently grow wealth.

Some things never change in the market. One of these things is the existence of great growth and recovery stories.

The biggest market secret is not that, given enough time, everything is cyclical.

It's not that "buy and hold forever" works or doesn't work depending on the different market environment.

It's not that the common wisdom of one investment era is terrible advice for another investment era.

It's not that every big market super-cycle lasts long enough for investors to forget what it felt like investing in the previous cycle.

It's not that every bubble has led to a deep correction, nor is it that every bust has set the foundations for another major uptrend.

It's not that the winners of each new bull market were always different than the ones from the previous bull market.

The biggest market secret is that the stock market has always been a market of stocks with huge divergence in the performance of individual equities.

No matter how the market averages perform over any 10-year period, there will always be individual stocks that will crush the averages.

The market is an opportunity machine.

TEN

8 to 80

"To make money in stocks you must have the vision to see them, the courage to buy them, and the patience to hold them. Patience is the rarest of the three."

— Thomas Phelps

"But there is only one side to the stock market, and it is not the bull side or the bear side, but the right side."

— Jesse Livermore

Let's Make a List

Over the next century there will be some incredible new and durable old trends that will deliver amazing opportunities for savvy investors.

We'll mine asteroids, robots will do most of our work, we'll interact with intelligent machines in various new ways, we'll travel to space, and we'll build cities on Mars. Biotech will change the way we do everything, and it will enhance our life exponentially.

All these trends — and some that may have yet to register — will create hundreds of stocks that will go up 1,000% or a lot more. And these profits will be there for the taking by anyone who knows how to grab them.

Some of these stocks will mature into what we call "8 to 80" companies and brands. They make products and provide services you'll use your whole life.

The simple way to understand "8 to 80" is as follows:

- When the markets are in turmoil, this is the list of companies where we go to shop.

- When the markets are trending up, these companies are the ones we're glad we own.

These companies will monetize major social and business trends over the long term. They have sustainable mass appeal — their reach is both broad and deep.

Our "8 to 80" portfolio includes stocks we plan to own for at least five years. We look for 20%-plus declines to establish new positions or add to existing ones.

Old School, New School

On February 2, 2017, Peter L. Brandt, one of the most successful and influential traders in the game today, posted this mind-blowing chart to the StockTwits community:

Figure 10-1

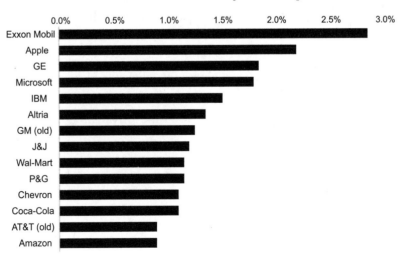

14 Stocks Account for 20% of U.S. Stock Gains
Percent of Market Wealth Creation From July 1926 through December 2015

Source: "Do Stocks Outperform Treasury Bills?" Hendrik Bessembinder

These 14 companies, as the graphic indicates, accounted for 20% of all wealth created by the stock market from July 1926 through December 2015.

Take a look at the names, listed in order of value created:

- Exxon Mobil
- Apple
- GE
- Microsoft
- IBM
- Altria
- GM (pre-2009 bailout)
- Johnson & Johnson
- Wal-Mart
- Procter & Gamble
- Chevron
- Coca-Cola
- AT&T (pre-1984 breakup)
- Amazon

These are all "8 to 80" companies and brands. They're profitable. They had huge moats for most of their life; some of them still do. And they're generally addictive and possibly evil.

Today our "8 to 80" list includes the following 14 companies, in alphabetical order:

- Alphabet (Google for search, YouTube for video)
- Amazon
- Apple
- Disney
- Facebook
- Federal Express
- Johnson & Johnson

- MasterCard
- Match Group
- Netflix
- Nike
- Starbucks
- Tencent Holdings
- Visa

They're profitable. They have huge moats. And they're generally addictive and possibly evil in new and different ways than the 20th century iteration of "8 to 80."

About Economic Moats

"Profitable" is self-explanatory: These companies all report positive earnings.

"Generally addictive and possibly evil" is a perception-and-value judgment. Take Facebook, for example.

There's a growing body of scientific literature devoted to the question of whether it's habit-forming.

As for "evil," well, to the extent it's replaced actual face-to-face human interaction with cyberfriendship, some might say it is. Has it turned fundamental human emotional connections into commodities?

That's a question for "Mr. Robot."

We're here to make investment decisions, not debate the social implications of emotion theft.

And Facebook is an "8 to 80" brand.

What's pretty clear to us is that even if we meet some Earth-shattering, economy-melting cataclysm, and everybody stops shopping on Amazon.com, kids as young as 8 and adults as old as 80 will be at home, posting memes and pictures, "Liking" some but not others, and roasting each other's political hot-takes, on Facebook.

Facebook now has more than 2 billion monthly users. Its 17% year-over-year growth rate is the fastest since 2012. As of mid-2017, 66% of monthly users were returning each day, up from 55% when it hit 1 billion users five years ago.

The product is basically complete, with innovation around the edges to keep users engaged. The user base is there, and it's growing.

Facebook has conquered its competition. YouTube has 1.5 billion users, WeChat 889 million. Twitter has 328 million, while Snapchat is estimated to have 255 million.

Other than YouTube, only Facebook's other apps have more than 1 billion users. That includes WhatsApp and Facebook Messenger, with 1.2 billion each. Instagram just crossed 700 million.

That's what we like to call an "economic moat," a concept created and made popular by Warren Buffet.

It describes a business's basic ability to maintain its competitive advantage, protect its long-term profits, and defend its market share.

In a 2007 talk to University of Florida MBA students the Sage of Omaha explained it this way:

> *I like businesses I can understand. We'll start with that. That narrows it down about 90%...There's all kinds of things I don't understand, but fortunately there's enough I do understand. You got this big, wide world out there. Almost every company is publicly owned...You got all American businesses, practically, available to you.*

> *Now, to start with, it doesn't make sense to go with things you think you can't understand. But you can understand some things. I can understand this [picks up can of Coca-Cola]. I mean, you can understand this. Anybody can understand this.*

> *I mean, this is a product that basically hasn't been changed much...since 1886...and it's a simple business. It's not an easy business. I don't want a business that's easy for competitors. I want a business with a moat around it. I want a very valuable castle in the middle. And then I want...the Duke who's in charge of that castle to be honest and hard-working and able. And then I want a big moat around the castle, and that moat can be various things.*

Amazon, for its part, has its own deep and wide defense against attack.

Amazon doesn't report Prime subscriber numbers. But a new line item in its annual report gives us pretty good insight into what's happening.

Its 10-K filing for 2016 noted $6.4 billion in revenue related to "retail subscription services." That doesn't seem like much for a company that generated total revenue of $136 billion last year. But it is a solid, recurring base, and it's growing.

We know Amazon charges $99 per year for an annual subscription and $10.99 per month for a monthly subscription. It also offers an $8.99-per-month Prime-Video-only plan.

One analyst, Robert Drbul of Guggenheim Securities, estimates a total of 65 million Prime subscribers. Another, John Blackledge of Cowen & Co., says the number is higher, about 80 million.

Consumer Intelligence Research Partners (CIRP) thinks the Prime ranks have doubled over the past couple years in the U.S. alone. CIRP's overall estimate is line with Blackledge's, at 80 million, with growth of nearly 40% over the past year.

That's 80 million U.S. households, or 60% of the total.

That, friends, is a helluvalotta "mind share." And that mind-dominance translates into wallet-share dominance.

We haven't even talked about Amazon Web Services, which might be the single most important piece of infrastructure in the ongoing 21st tech boom.

These are the servers that power Netflix, Instagram, countless government websites, and start-ups all over the map. Walmart is already bullying its partners to get off of Amazon's cloud.

Amazon is also at the forefront of artificial intelligence, machine learning, and drone technology.

Even Nike has capitulated...Nike thought its moat was "cool products." Its products are cool.

But when people consider buying stuff — cool books, cool music, cool movies, cool products of any kind, including shoes and fashology, they think about Amazon.

With its "obsessive customer focus," Amazon has won the battle for mind share.

Its moat is big and growing.

I'm Glad You Asked...

"8 to 80" is the answer to the question, "How do we build a great list of stocks to watch and own if we don't really care much about trading or watching the markets?"

We like to invest in growth companies, but the fact is they're crowded.

They're crowded because they're easier to spot. And they're crowded because money is paid nothing to sit on the sidelines.

Our "8 to 80" list has evolved over the past year, and we continue to tinker with it.

If you invest or trade, it's very important to keep moving forward, to reserve some capital so you can live another day, and to remember that everyone has their "if onlys."

Our current list doesn't include any names specifically tied to the cybersecurity trend, for example.

We also lack direct exposure to software-as-a-service (SaaS), though perhaps our focus on Google and Microsoft is sufficient. You could make a similar case for automation, artificial intelligence, and robotics, where Google's X unit is doing some heavy R&D.

We did drop two stocks over the last 12 months, Under Armour and Tesla. Under Armour simply doesn't rise to the level of the other companies in the current list, including Nike, which, along with Apple, dominates the "fashology" space. We dropped Tesla because it remains unprofitable.

Match Group and Tencent Holdings are new to the list. Match Group is edgy.

It hasn't been public very long, but it controls the online dating world. And Tencent is just so dominant in China in mobile and payments.

No index or list is perfect.

Our current "8 to 80" list looks different than what it would have 30 years ago because the market is constantly changing. Edges come and go. Moats don't last forever, but, in some cases, they can last a very long time and make investors a lot of money. We're interested in long-term moats.

The "8 to 80" list will keep evolving. The secret sauce over time is not so much the list itself but the ability to adjust, reallocate, and manage risk as we go.

How to Buy

Undiscovered and under-followed momentum leaders are best bought first on strength after they break out from a strong base (a tight price range area). You can add to them on pullbacks to their rising 10-, 20-, and 50-day moving averages depending on the market.

But large-cap, over-followed stocks with strong moats — our "8 to 80" brands — are better bought on weakness.

If you're not already in them, wait for a 10% to 20% market correction or pullbacks to their respective rising 100- and 200-day moving averages. You can subsequently add to your position on a breakout from a strong technical base.

Yes, Amazon might be eventually going to $2,000 in the next three to five years. But if you chase it and get a sloppy entry, you'll get shaken out on a normal 5% to 10% market selloff.

Anyone can find a potential big winner. Not everyone can stay in it long enough to make a real difference in their returns. The real difference comes from something we call "holding power."

The right entry and the right position size give you holding power. They let you ride normal market fluctuations without losing your mind, and they keep you from selling when you probably need to be buying.

Buying *right* matters.

Get in the Game

We've seen and/or experienced four major panics and crashes over the past 30 years: the 1987 "Black Monday" moment; the 1998 Asian contagion/Long-Term Capital Management crisis; the 2000 internet bubble burst; and the Global Financial Crisis/Great Recession of 2008-09.

All of them were messy, and all of them caused great pain. But all of them created massive new opportunities for investors with a plan — for investors with a list.

The stock market can be a fun and profitable place if you take the time to learn its language, establish a repeatable strategy, and exercise strict discipline.

Preserve capital in bad markets, and you'll live to ride the next great trends, which are always around the corner.

The market, in other words, is an opportunity machine.

You don't have to watch every financial talk show, catch every move, understand every sector, or follow every narrative.

Nobody really knows anything, but that's how and why they fill up CNBC and Bloomberg television and reams of bogus brokerage research.

In fact, most of the time, the markets and stocks come back to you. And, most of the time, bad things happen when you chase markets and stocks.

We're always willing to let an investment become a trade, but we resist letting a trade become an investment.

If a market or stock gives you a gain in two days you would have been happy with in two years, it's OK to change your timeframe.

The beauty of the market is that we don't need to know which technologies are going to change the world and which companies are going to benefit the most.

The market will tell you which stocks to buy and when to buy them.

All you need to do is to listen.

We hope the ideas offered in this book serve as a guide for you.

You should always think for yourself and take every opinion with a grain of salt. In this case it's obvious that we're biased.

Our financial research business and our personal market approaches are based on the deeply ingrained belief that markets are inefficient and can be beaten with proper equity selection and risk management.

We're not telling you to stop dollar-cost averaging in low-fee index funds so you can start learning how to pick stocks.

We're just sharing what has worked for us and where we'll continue to focus our efforts.

ABOUT THE AUTHORS

Howard Lindzon has more than 20 years' experience in the financial community acting in both an entrepreneurial and investing capacity. With a unique vision for starting, managing, and successfully advising innovative companies, Lindzon is the public-face of the Social Leverage entities.

In 2008 Lindzon co-founded StockTwits, where he invented the "cashtag." StockTwits was recently named "one of the top 10 most innovative companies in web" by FastCompany and one of the "50 best websites" by Time.

Previously, Lindzon created more than 400 original videos on Wallstrip, acquired by CBS in 2007. Lindzon stepped down from his operational role as CEO of StockTwits on December 31, 2013, to focus on the next phase of Social Leverage. As acting Chairman, Lindzon's connection to StockTwits, along with his hedge fund experience, give Social Leverage access to a community of professionals who can evaluate fintech opportunities.

Follow him on Twitter and StockTwits @howardlindzon and at howardlindzon.com.

Ivaylo Ivanov is a full-time trader.

Ivaylo is a founder of MarketWisdom. com, where he offers mentorship and market education on swing trading and momentum investing.

He is the author of *Top 10 Trading Setups: How to Find Them, How to Manage Them, How to Make Money with Them, Crash: How to Protect*

and Grow Capital during Corrections, *The 5 Secrets to Highly Profitable Swing Trading*, and *The StockTwits Edge: 40 Setups from Real Market Pros*.

Ivaylo's work has been featured on *Bloomberg News*, *The Wall Street Journal*, *Yahoo! Finance*, *Reuters*, *CNN Money*, *UT San Diego*, *Traders Magazine*, *Abnormal Returns* (www.abnormalreturns.com), *Real Clear Markets* (www.realclearmarkets.com), *The Reformed Broker* (www.thereformedbroker.com), and *Zero Hedge* (www.zerohedge.com), among other widely followed financial media.

You can follow him on Twitter and StockTwits @ivanhoff and at ivanhoff.com and marketwisdom.com.

DISCLAIMER

The views expressed in this book are the personal views of the authors only and do not necessarily reflect the views of the authors' employers. The views expressed reflect the current views of authors as of the date hereof and the authors do not undertake to advise you of any changes in the views expressed herein. In addition, the views expressed do not necessarily reflect the opinions of any investment professional at the authors' employers, and may not be reflected in the strategies and products that their employers offer. The authors' employers may have positions (long or short) or engage in securities transactions that are not consistent with the information and views expressed in this presentation. The authors assume no duty to nor undertake to update forward-looking statements. No representation or warranty, express or implied, is made or given by or on behalf of the authors, the authors' employers or any other person as to the accuracy and completeness or fairness of the information contained in this presentation and no responsibility or liability is accepted for any such information. By accepting this book, the recipient acknowledges its understanding.